Entering Rest
Be Still

A 40-Day Journey into the Presence of God

by

Cheryl and Harry Salem

Unless otherwise indicated, all scripture quotations are taken from the New Spirit-Filled Life® Bible. Copyright © 2002 by Thomas Nelson, Inc. Used by permission. Scripture within text appears in italics.

Second Printing

Entering Rest – Be Still
A 40-Day Journey into the Presence of God
ISBN 1-890370-20-7

Copyright© 2012, by Salem Family Ministries
PO Box 701287
Tulsa, OK 74170

Published by Salem Family Ministries
PO Box 701287
Tulsa, OK 74170

Dedication

Dear _____,

I dedicate this book to you. I pray that you
lose yourself in the love of God as you give yourself
entirely to the discovery of true rest.
May this journey bring you into a deeper and more
intimate walk with your heavenly Father.
You will never be the same.

I love you,

_____

Signed

_____

Date

Acknowledgement

This book has not been without much effort, prayer, and time spent, being still and praying, listening and hearing from heaven. After the message is received, and then written, the real fun begins! The book then has to be read, and re-read, edited, and re-edited, many times over until we feel we have 'caught' every error.

To our dear friends, Diana, Richard, & Kari: Thank you for your help in getting this book printed, and for being covenant partners with our ministry. You are all precious to us. We love you and we thank God for you. May you continue to rest in God's grace and provision.

As always, many thanks goes to Tracey Jacobs who has been working alongside Harry, Harry III, Roman and me in this family ministry for twenty-two years. She is faithful, and chosen by God to stand with us. Whatever we need, no matter how great or how small, she is always ready to do what is necessary. She has been stretched way beyond her comfort zone by the Lord, and has done whatever we have needed through the years, including learning how to lay out manuscripts, edit, typeset (if it is still called that anymore!), do the cover design, all while on her knees with much prayer and intercession going forth. Tracey, words will never express our heartfelt thanks to you for all your hard work, and loving efforts. We know you do it unto the Lord, therefore, we expect many jewels in your eternal crown for the multitude of lives who will be forever changed because of your gifts and talents laid at His feet. Thank you.

We thank God for every hand put forth in bringing this revelation into being. God knows every person by name.

We love you and thank God for you,

Cheryl & Harry Salem

Contents

Contents

"Rest"

True rest that we long for, the very longing of our deepest soul... that rest is found hidden inside HIM.
It isn't just something to be found inside Him; the rest we long for 'IS HIM.'

Entering Rest
Be Still

All of humanity experiences a hunger, a thirst for deeper purpose and meaning of life. This hunger is driving many to seek what, who, how to quench this deepest need. Are you pursuing something or someone to fulfill the immense void within your own heart? If you can honestly answer, "Yes, I need fulfillment; I long to have these desires met! I desire acceptance without judgment, love without criticism, and even things that cannot be uttered, or even known by my conscious mind to be filled with something much greater than a human hand, or even a human heart!" If this is you, then our pursuit is the same.

As I become wiser with the years, (that's a feminine way of saying that I am getting older!), I am beginning to realize that many things I spent much time thinking, pondering, meditating on, giving much time and attention to were quite useless and not of any real eternal value. Please don't get me wrong. I am not saying that what we have done or maybe what you have done has not been fruitful. On the contrary, what all of us have been so diligently doing, as in our case for decades, has had some effect on the kingdom of God. But in the eternal scheme of things, from an eternal perspective, have we wasted much time 'doing, doing, doing,' when, could it be possible that the Spirit of God may have simply been calling us to a place of rest at His feet?

If there are lives changed, and souls for eternity with God because of our much doing then this fruit will remain, and that is cause for celebration. But if we truly examine ourselves and check the sincere motivation of our hearts on many things we have spent hours, days, weeks, and even years of our time, attention, and resources doing, if it is not producing souls for the kingdom of God, if it is not snatching lives out of the grip of darkness, then in the eternal scheme of things, has it been worth it? For when the fire of God cascades down to bring about the last great outpouring of purification, what of all that we have done will still be standing?

This has been a season like no other, and God has been amazing through it all. In thirty years of ministry I have never known a place, a time, a season like the one we are in right now. There is a tangible presence of God that is wooing us, calling us inside Himself. If we do not listen, then we will not hear. If we do not look, then we will not see. If we do not open our hearts to let it be given, then we will not receive. This is not something that can be physically 'done,' but it's more of a willingness on our part to 'be.' What am I writing about? The impartation of this book can be life-changing, heart-rearranging, and most accurately, a way of thinking unlike anything we have ever known before. I have literally had to stop myself from my old ways of thinking to be able to get any comprehension on this much deeper place inside God, eternal Creator, deepest, highest, richest, beyond our imagination bridegroom who loves us!

The eternal lover of our souls is saying to those of us who are listening, "Be still, and know Me." The highest place we can attain within our relationship with the eternal lover of our souls is being required of us. The bridegroom is demanding His bride to come forth and be made ready. There is no more time left to simply talk the talk of 'lover of the Lord.' There is a timeline, a deadline, if you will, of preparation and preparedness that is upon us. We are about to stand before all of heaven to be examined and we will either be found ready or not ready. Which one are you? Hopefully, this book will help you examine your own heart, mind, and daily life to determine where you actually stand in the 'readiness' position for the bridegroom's return.

We have been getting clearer instructions from the Lord. Some are not 'earth-shattering' revelations for anyone except us personally, but to hear His voice and to know His direction for our next steps is so wonderful. And yet, even when I write these words, I find it difficult to adequately put these new revelations by the Spirit of God into words. Things of the Spirit of God are dimensional beyond what can be diluted into words and pages. These things are seen, heard, and mostly experienced with all realms of who we are: spirit, soul, and body.

To walk in the fullness of who God has created us to be, not just to do, but to be, we must experience God in dimensions where our own natural mind will not want to equate. The natural mind cannot take the things of the Spirit and slot them mentally into a place of quick understanding, neither can this last days' bride of Christ. We can no longer mentally assent to this purification process that is mandatory for us to be made ready for His impartation of who He is into our being. It is not as much about *understanding mentally* as it is about *receiving spiritually.*

We are a generation who loves the 'how-to' manual. We love to be told what to do and how to do it. We are much like the children of Israel when they demanded instructions/rules in place of personal relationship based upon deep trust and intimacy. The Lord is calling us to a place of complete and total denial of 'self.' It is not something that can be laid down in steps 1 through 10. It is a daily walk, a constant, never-ending discovery, a never actually arriving, journey of intimacy.

Instead of trying to put intimate, heartfelt expressions into mere words, let's take a journey through this book into the very essence and intimate places of the heart of God. For those of you who approach your relationship with God Almighty through an intellectual sphere, you will probably be lost from the beginning. God does not need our thoughts, we need His. God does not need our rules, laws, or how-to's of entering into His presence. He needs our willingness to abandon ourselves at His feet without time constraints, lists, thoughts of places to be, and things to see and do!

To 'be still' in His presence and to know what He is saying is so precious but it does not come easy. For many of us to 'come' to the place He is calling us is the highest and most difficult place of obedience we have known to this point. There are changes coming on the horizon of God's kingdom. He is getting ready to return for His bride. For years, we have known a part of our calling has been to prepare the bride. We know this, and see it clearly. His church, His bride, His body are being made ready.

Being prepared can be and usually is painful at times. It feels like being in the Lord's 'boot camp.' Could this be a part of the 'fire of God' being poured out upon us for purification and preparation? I know that the season of preparation is here now. *It is not coming ... it is here.* It is upon us. Will you enter into His presence with us through these coming days and weeks? Are you ready to abandon all self-promotion, priorities, prizes, dreams, visions, hopes? Are you ready to deny yourself those 'safe places' where hidden sins and "What about me?" thoughts have been lord and king in your thinking? There can be no more "What about me?" when all has been abandoned for "What about Him?" Can you come with me? More importantly, will you come with me?

Everything in God is seasonal. This is a season like our generation has not known before. I see by my spirit that the body of Christ has tried to run ahead and not listen to Him as He has pulled on the reins of our necks to slow down, listen, sit at His feet, learn of Him, and be totally led of Him. This is a word for us all, for the last days' bride, the last days' church, His body.

There are some things that must be laid down to accomplish this call of God that is upon us now. But we must not neglect our time alone in His Word, listening, learning, being renewed and refreshed ... being still. This is a command, not a request, and if we do not obey, we will not be ready when the trumpet sounds. It does not matter how many times we have prayed the 'prayer,' or confessed our sins. What will tell the absolute truth in our lives is the level of preparation and purification we have endured to be made in His image. He is coming for a bride that is His image, not some human idea of what His bride will look like. His bride will not be a 'look.' His bride will be Him, personified in the body of His feminine bride.

Rest can only be found when it is not about 'us' any longer. True rest that we long for, the very longing of our deepest soul ... that rest is found hidden inside Him. It isn't *just* something to be found inside Him, the rest we long for *is Him*.

As long as I stand alone, I struggle to 'do' all the things necessary to be accepted. When I finally abandon my desires to 'do' and accept the wooing of my ultimate soulmate, the lover of my very soul, Jesus Christ, my bridegroom, I can 'be-come' His image ... nothing of me left. All of Christ is showing through me, His image, His desire, His longing.

Ultimately, when Christ went to the cross and endured the pain and suffering that was upon Him, He did it for the joy that was set before Him. (Hebrews 12:2) What joy is that? Maybe the question is not what but who? The joy that was set before Him then, was me, and you! He looked into the future and He saw His bride waiting for Him. At the end of this journey of entering rest, you should be able to say, "He endured over 2,000 years ago for me. I was the joy set before Him then, and I am the joy set before Him now. I am His joy, and He is mine!"

...and the Spirit and the Bride say "Come!" And let him who hears say, "Come!" And let him who thirsts come. Whoever desires, let him take the water of life freely. (Revelation 22:17)

I am the bride and I say to the Lord, my bridegroom, "Come, Lord Jesus!"

Entering Rest
Be Still

We've designed this book to be used one of two ways. You can pray and journal for yourself, creating a very personal and intimate diary between yourself and God. Or, if you have someone specific in mind, you can dedicate this book to them, committing to 40 days of prayer and journaling on their behalf, and then give them this book, with your heartfelt journal notes included, as a very special gift.

Regardless of how this book is used, it's not a book you can 'do' on the run! In fact, it's the opposite. You must sit down, be still, and 'come away with the lover of your soul,' to fulfill the purpose within these pages. We have segmented this book for convenience and understanding.

Each day there will be *knowledge* for you to obtain in regard to rest; then *ownership* which is a prayer section for you; then the *action* section, which is a prayer written out with blanks for you to fill in with either your own name or the name of a friend or loved one as you pray for them!

Then each day, the last section is a place for you to be quiet and listen to the Holy Spirit. As you learn to pray and communicate with God, listen to His voice and journal what He gives you! This can change your prayer life!

Once you have finished the last pages, we pray you have not learned how to 'do,' but rather how to 'be still' and know that He is your God. This is a time of ...

Entering Rest!

Day One

Psalm 46:10-11
Be still, and know that I am God; I will be exalted among the nations, I will be exalted in the earth! The Lord of Hosts is with us; The God of Jacob is our refuge. Selah

Knowledge:

'To be' rather than 'to do,' that is the real question, isn't it? And truly spoken, it should be 'to be' first then 'to do.' The crucial statement of our hearts is to be hidden in Christ, to be crucified with Christ, to be identified in Christ. Throughout the scriptures, God's Word is plain that we are 'to be.' We are to 'be saved.' We are to 'be healed,' 'be reconciled to Christ,' 'be filled with the Holy Spirit' and to 'be made ready.' There is such an overwhelming push through God's Word to be, to become, not to settle in and stay the way we are but to 'be changed' in the likeness and image of God!

> *Just be still, and know that He is God.*

Once we truly give our lives to Christ, we can begin to grow and mature inside of Christ Jesus' body. We are a part of Him and should not stunt the growth of the body of Christ by our unwillingness to grow up! My entire life has been identified by my much doing, but God by His Spirit has brought me into a place where 'being' has become the focus of my future rather than being identified with what I do, with my works for God. Jesus Christ is requiring me to be identified with Him.

Today, let's take the time to *be still and know that He is God.* Let's be still and know Him. Simply to 'be still' is a huge challenge for some of us. I challenge you today to stop moving, doing, running. Stop your mind from racing away after only a few moments in God's presence. Come to His feet today with 'no agenda,' simply to 'be still.' I think you will be amazed at how quickly you realize how your heart has longed for His presence. Be still and listen to His voice.

Ownership:

Father, I come before You to simply 'be still.' I want to know that You are God, and not just God of the universe, but my God, my personal God. I know by Your Word that You will be exalted among the nations, and that You will be exalted in the earth, and I want part of that exaltation to come through me as I am being still at Your feet. Forgive me, Lord, when I run around sometimes without thoughts of You. Forgive me when I focus more on what I am doing, than who I am being. Teach me, Lord, as I discipline myself over the coming weeks to be still, how to enjoy Your presence without agendas, lists, or performances. You are the Lord of hosts, and You are with me. You are the God of Jacob, and You are my God, also. You are my refuge, and I run to You to sit at Your feet and be still. Selah, I will pause and calmly think on this and meditate on Your Word throughout the day, in Jesus' name. Amen.

Action:

Lord, I thank You that ___I am___ ~~is~~ learning to be still, and in that position ___I___ will learn that You are truly God. I ask that You exalt Yourself through ___my___ ~~'s~~ life. Lord, may ___I___ know that You are the Lord of hosts and that You are with ~~(him/her.)~~ me You are the God of Jacob, and You are ___my___ ~~'s~~ refuge. Selah, ___I___ will pause and calmly think on this and meditate on Your Word today. I declare this in Jesus' name. Amen.

Be Still ...

Journal your deepest thoughts while you pray. God is listening and He wants to talk to you.

I don't know how to pray a lot of times. Sometimes I feel like my prayers are always saying the same thing and the words don't come as smoothly as other people's words when they pray in a group setting.

I know you know my heart. I ask that you continue to bring the right words to my heart whenever I pray

Thank you, Lord. I know you are with me always.

"Selah"

Stop!
Pause and calmly
think of that.

Day Two

Psalm 4:3-4
But know that the Lord has set apart for Himself him who is godly; The Lord will hear when I call to Him.
Be angry, and do not sin. Meditate within your heart on your bed, and be still. Selah

Knowledge:

Selah is a term that means to *stop! Pause, and calmly think of that*. When we see this word, *"Selah"* in the Bible it is a command for us to stop doing what we are doing, including reading. We are to stop reading and think about what we just read. We are to meditate on it, mulling it over and over in our minds throughout the day until the very thought has become a part of our being. After we have done the above we can truly say to the Lord, "I got it."

"Lord, I hear You calling me and I am listening..."

Being still, learning to mediate and listen to His still, small voice is a huge part of entering into His ordained rest in our daily lives. Rest is not a pill we can take or a special 'rest drink' to whip up in the blender with 'rest powder - just add milk.' No, the rest we long for, this rest of God can only be entered through willfully bringing our physical bodies, our minds, our emotions, and our spirits into a subjective place under the presence and power of our loving and yet Almighty Father God.

I choose to be still today and listen. Would you choose that and then do it with me? Simply lie down, or sit down, breathe deeply of His presence all around you. Listen to

His still, quiet, whispering voice. He is calling you, wooing you into a place of His rest, just for you.

God loves you more than you can imagine. With your spirit eyes, try to see His arms outstretched to you, bidding you to jump up in His lap as He pulls you close to his chest to hold you securely. Shhhhh ... He whispers ... *be still.*

Ownership:

I know the Lord has set me apart for Himself, because I have chosen to walk in Him, and through Him. Because of Christ's redemption plan that I have received for myself, I am godly through Christ. I know the Lord hears me when I call to Him. When I am angry, I will myself through the power of the cross of Christ to not step over into sin. I choose to put a watch over my mouth and a guard over my heart. I do not allow my flesh to rise up and cause me to sin. I am a spirit housed in flesh, not the other way around. I will meditate in my heart on my bed, and I will be still. I will pause, and contemplate the outcome of actions and reactions when angry, and I will calm down. Thank You, Lord, that You are teaching me how to walk each day, under control, by the Spirit of Jesus Christ within me, in Jesus' name. Amen.

Action:

Lord, I know You have set apart ___me___ for Your-self. ___I have___ ~~has~~ chosen to walk in You, and through You because of Your redemption plan that (he/she) has received. ___I am___ ~~is~~ godly through Christ. You hear ___me___ when (~~he/she~~) calls to You. When ___I am___ is angry, ___I___ will choose to not step over into sin, through the power of the cross of Christ. ___I___ chooses to put a watch over (his/her) mouth and a guard over (his/her) heart. ___I do___ ~~does~~ not allow flesh to rise up and cause (him/her) to sin. ___I am___ ~~is~~ a spirit living in flesh, not the other way around. ___I___ will meditate in (his/her) heart on (his/her) bed, and be still. ___I___ will pause, and contemplate the outcome of actions and reactions when angry. ___I___ will calm down. Thank You, Lord, that You are teaching ___me___ to walk each day controlled by the Spirit of Jesus Christ within (him/her), in Jesus' name. Amen.

Shhhh ...

Can you hear
Him calling you
to come to Him,
to rest and be still?

Be still ...

Journal your thoughts as you pray and be still before the Lord. He is the Word, therefore He has much to say to you and through you. Be still and listen. Take the time to write it down.

I am not a good journaler, I never have been. But I will take this time to do what I can and ask God to help me understand more about Him as I try to journal.

Nehemiah 8:11

"Be still,
for the day
is holy."

Day Three

Nehemiah 8:10-11
Then he said to them, "Go your way, eat the fat, drink the sweet, and send portions to those for whom nothing is pre-pared; for this day is holy to our Lord. Do not sorrow, for the joy of the Lord is your strength. So the Levites qui-eted all the people, saying, "Be still, for the day is holy; do not be grieved."

Knowledge:
The joy of the Lord is our strength. What a wonderful statement! When we focus on three words in these two verses it's quite interesting how they fit together like pieces of a puzzle. Joy... Strength... (Be) Still.

We want to have strength to go through life without quit-ting. We want to go through everyday life with joy, too. But notice the command from the priests (Levites) to *"Be still."* We cannot find our joy or our strength by running around like a chicken with its head cut off! (If you have never seen a chicken run around without its head, it's not pretty!)

If we want the joy of the Lord and the strength of the Lord in our daily lives, we must discipline ourselves to be still and simply be in His pres-ence. In His presence is the only place *"fullness of joy"* can be found. Psalm 16:11 states, *"You will show me the path of life; In Your presence is fullness of joy; At Your right hand are pleasures forevermore."*

> *Discipline produces a harvest!*
> Hebrews 12:11 (NIV)

Type A's, listen up! Here's a list! First, we must learn to be content in the very presence of God, who must be Lord of our lives. Second, we must take care of those around us, for whom nothing is prepared. It's not too hard in our present day economy to find widows, orphans, and families struggling all around us. When we have enough, the Lord says send out of our portions to those with no portions. Third, we are to rejoice. We are to be all about Him, and stop feeling sorry for ourselves. To do this we must take our eyes off ourselves, and keep our eyes completely on Him. These are easy words to say, but not so easy to do!

When I see the phrase, *"do not sorrow,"* I think of when our children were smaller and throughout every day they would do those things that did not please me as a mama. When I would correct them they learned quickly to say, "Mama, I am sorry." I got so tired of hearing, "I'm sorry, I'm sorry, I'm sorry." I got to the point when the children would say, "Mama, I'm sorry," I would immediately respond, "Don't be sorry, be different."

Now I sigh a long, slow sigh even as I write this, because I remember hearing the Lord repeat my words back to me many times as I would say them to the children. His still, small voice would whisper in my ear, "Okay, if that's the way you want to play. Cheryl, stop coming to Me with 'I'm sorry.' Don't be sorry, be different." Oh, how those words sounded harsh coming back at me! But even today, when I read those simple words, *"do not sorrow,"* I hear the Lord say, "Don't be sorry, be different."

Don't be sorry - be different.

Now that I am older, I realize that to say words like, "I'm sorry," is much easier than 'being different.' Saying the words is easier than living the life, but the Lord is requiring us to learn how to live the life of joy and strength, not in our own abilities, but inside of His very presence. Can you hear Him whisper in your own ear? He is saying, "Come away with Me, and be still. I will do what is necessary to cause you to have joy and strength."

Relax, and enjoy His presence. No one loves you more, or thinks you are more wonderful, than the One who has created you. The Lord created within each one of us a void. There is that deep void inside each one of us that the Lord God Himself put there. Why would He do such a thing to us? Because He put a void in us that can only be filled by Him. He wants us to spend our lives searching for Him, the only One who can fill the void of desire, pleasure, passion, joy, and strength. He is all those things, and He is the only One who can fill, and fulfill those things, those voids in our own lives. Will you come away with Him right now, with no agenda, just to be together? He has great pleasure just being with you. Take a few moments to breathe in the depths of His presence... He is here, waiting for you.

Ownership:

Lord, today I will go about my regular daily routine of life. I will enjoy without guilt those things You have blessed me with, and I will share portions of my blessings from You with those around me who do not yet have these wonderful blessings. I know that this day and every day is holy, dedicated, and set apart for You. Because of that, I will not sorrow, and I will watch and pray to not be so sorry either. I ask You, Lord, to teach me to stop certain behavior before I do it, so I do not have to repent later and say, "I'm sorry." Out of this effort, I will learn that Your joy is my strength. When I hear the voice of Your servant tell me to settle down, or when the still, small voice of Your presence says for me to quiet down and be still, I will listen and obey. I declare that I know this day is holy unto You, Lord, and I will not be grieved over the past, but I look to the future with Your strength and Your joy, in Jesus' name. Amen.

Action:

Lord, I bring to Your feet my beloved _____. As (he/she) goes about (his/her) daily life, I ask that You reveal Your presence to (him/her). I thank You, Lord, that _____ is learning to enjoy You, and to not feel guilty about the blessings and pleasures You have given (him/her). I thank You, Lord, that _____ is generous and shares portions of blessings with those who do not have any portions. Thank You, Lord, that _____ knows and recognizes that this day and every day is holy and dedicated to You. I thank You, that _____ is set apart for You and Your pleasure. _____ will not sorrow, but will be strengthened and overjoyed by Your presence. When You, Holy Spirit, speak to (his/her) heart, _____ will hear and obey and be still. _____ will not be grieved, in Jesus' name. Amen.

Be still ...

There is no better way to hear His voice than to be still. Do not surround yourself with noise today, but be quiet, and listen. Don't be afraid to take the time to write what you hear from the throne of God. He longs to be with you. He longs to talk to you. Will you listen?

Don't be sorry, be different.
Lord, help me to practice this
first so I can be an
example to Andriana in
it.

Day Four

Isaiah 28:12
"This is the resting place, let the weary rest" (NIV)

Knowledge:

Rest! What a powerful and yet simple word. We all think we know what it means, but what if we have lost something in translation? I believe we have done just that! Let's examine from where the word *rest* has originated. In the *Strong's Concordance*[1], this word is found as #4496 and is Hebrew in origin. It is spelled *menuchah* and is pronounced (meh-noo-chah).

According to the Word Wealth section found in the Spirit-Filled Life Bible at Isaiah 28:12, *menuchah* means *resting place; place of stillness, repose, consolation, peace, rest; a quiet place; also the condition of restfulness. Menuchah* is derived from the Hebrew word *nuach*. This is a verb which means *to rest, soothe, settle down, comfort.* Because Noah's parents could foresee the comfort that his life would bring (Genesis 5:29) they named him Noah. This name is derived from the root word *nuach.* Isaiah 28:12 states, *"This is the resting place, let the weary rest."* So for us to apply this word in our conversation to one another I would say to you, "Please enter into menuchah." In that simple statement, I would be pronouncing a blessing upon you of rest. *Menuchah* could mean *a place, a mental attitude, an emotional position of great soothing, comfort, and settling down.* For many it would mean a physical halting of movement to begin the mental, and emotional halting of busy-ness.

So this is what we long for to replace the stressful hustle-bustle of this life. And if this is what we long for, then why do we continue pushing, shoving, moving in and through each and every day with so much busy, busy, busy, stress, stress, stress!? Starting for many is difficult but stopping seems to be even more difficult for our generation. To simply slow down and stop the "merry-go-round" cycle in which we seem to find ourselves, there is a key element which must be dealt with in each of our lives. TRUST. I have literally stared at this word until I noticed the simplicity of it. There is a cross (the letter 't') on each end, and then 'us' is in the middle. I think that fairly sums up the true meaning of the word 'trust' in a person's life. We must truly meet Christ at His cross, where 'me' becomes 'us.' Then we take up our own cross and follow Him. Trust is the key that can bring us to this place called *menuchah* described in Psalm 23:2-3, (my translation) *He leads me (and I follow Him) beside the waters of menuchah, still waters, the waters of quietness. In this place where He leads and I follow, my soul is restored.*

Ownership:

Father, I approach Your throne asking that I may rest in Your resting place. There are times, sometimes even days that I am weary, and can't seem to get myself to a place of rest. I realize that it is not in my own human ability to 'find rest' and obtain it apart from who You are. Therefore, as I come before You today I ask that I may enter into You; You are my resting place, and in You I can rest. Thank You, Lord for the rest that only You can give me. I receive it into my life today and always. I thank You, Lord, for You are my rest, in Jesus' name I pray. Amen.

Action:

Father, there are so many things, people, places, stresses, distractions all around us each day. I bring _____ to Your throne today, Lord, and I ask that _____ may enter into Your rest for (him/her). There are times when weariness becomes acceptable in our lives as we get used to feeling weary, but Lord, I ask that _____ recognize the weariness of (his/her) soul, and I ask that You draw _____ to You. Lord, You are the resting place that _____ longs for, and only in You can true rest be found. Thank You, Lord, that You are _____'s resting place and in You, _____ can find rest, in Jesus' name. Amen.

Be still ...
Pray and journal as you listen to His voice.

_____
_____
_____
_____
_____
_____
_____
_____
_____
_____
_____
_____
_____
_____
_____
_____
_____
_____
_____
_____
_____
_____
_____
_____
_____
_____
_____
_____
_____

"Rest"

Hebrew translation:
"menuchah"

A resting place; place of stillness,
repose, consolation, peace, rest;
a quiet place; also the condition
of restfulness.

Entering Rest

Day Five

Hebrews 4:1, 11-12
Therefore, since a promise remains of entering His rest,
let us fear lest any of you seem to have come short of it.
Let us therefore be diligent to enter that rest, lest anyone
fall according to the same example of disobedience.
For the word of God is living and powerful, and sharper
than any two-edged sword, piercing even to the division of
soul and spirit, and of joints and marrow, and is a dis-
cerner of the thoughts and intents of the heart.

Knowledge:

Rest is a word we speak of many times, but very few have ever learned how to truly and successfully *rest in the Lord,* nor do we ever consider the ramifications of disobeying the Lord by not resting when He calls us into that place. When the Lord gives us specific scriptures, as He has above, that remind us of His promise of rest, and then a warning that we should be afraid to disobey Him in this, shouldn't we obey? Yes, and without hesitation! We are not to fall short of entering into His rest; we are to be diligent and one translation uses the phrase that we are to *labor* to enter into the promise of rest. So if rest is promised and that promise still holds today, as the Message Bible translation says it does (read Hebrews 4), then why are we as a society, the church, as families, marriages, a community, a nation, and the world moving at such a fast pace?

To enter into God's promised rest for us is not a sentence to be quoted, a statement to be made, a 'hotel' to check in to, but it is a lifelong pursuit, a journey, a destination to be attained over time. But even in our pursuit of rest, we must never forget that it is not a place; rest is not a where, or even a what. Rest is a 'who.' Rest is found inside of Him who is our refuge, our strength, our resting and hiding place, Jesus Christ. I can rest when I am hidden in Him. So can you! You can find this place of rest, no matter what is going on around you, when you run to His feet, and hide yourself inside Him. There you can find the rest your heart longs for, your mind is desperate for, and your body must have to survive the onslaught of the enemy all around us.

For me, it is sometimes found when I first do the simplest of things, when I make a physical choice, a physical action of laboring to rest. But mostly, it is a mental exercise of stilling the mind, not letting my thoughts wander off in every direction. We can will our thoughts to be still and rest at the feet of our Master, Jesus Christ.

> *I choose to enter into His rest today.*

Entering into God's kind of rest is not just the absence of chaos and stress, but more of a positioning of our own choices to make Jesus Christ the King of all areas of our destiny. To take rest as our possession we must first realize that it is a promise of God for us. Rest has already been given, but the Bible says, *"only a few will enter in,"* to that promise of rest.

Why would we not accept the promise of rest from the King of Kings? Maybe because we do not understand that we can't obtain it on our own, but must accept it as our gift from the only One who can truly give it to us? He gives us access through Himself, to enter rest.

I choose to allow the Word of God to discern my heart,

my intentions, and my purpose. When we get too busy to read our Bibles, too busy to pray, too busy to be still and listen, too busy to rest, we have chosen to ignore one of God's best promises for us. Won't you enter into His rest with me?

Ownership:

Lord, I admit and ask You to forgive me when I have run ahead of Your voice. Forgive me when I try to do things on my own, when I try to please You through my much doing, rather than learn who I really am at Your feet. I recognize that You promised me rest and in that promise I can be free from the things I cannot control! Lord, I long to please You, therefore, I will enter into Your rest and not look back to my old ways of doing things. I will accept Your promise and because of Your love for me, I choose to do what it takes to enter into rest and learn to live inside Your rest.

I will be diligent to enter Your promise and because of my position inside of Your promise, I will not fall because of disobedience. I will stand in Your promise because of obedience. I submit myself to Your Word which is alive and powerful. Lord, Your Word is sharper than any two-edged sword dividing my soul and spirit, my joints and marrow! I thank You, Lord, that Your Word divides between the pure and impure, the righteous and the unrighteous inside me, therefore I hide myself inside of You. Thank You, Father, that the more I learn to rest in You, the more You will separate from me what needs to be gone, and show me what I need to repent of, and I will be set free as I am hidden in You. Lord, Your Word is the discerner of my heart and my thoughts, and I thank You, that as I rest in You I will be able to trust You more and more. Forgive me when I don't trust You, for You are altogether trustworthy. Thank

You for trusting me for I am not trustworthy but still, You love me. Lord, I trust You. Help me to trust You more, in Jesus' name I pray. Amen.

Action:

Lord, I thank You that _____ recognizes and chooses to enter into Your promise of rest. Lord, help _____ to understand the ramifications of disobeying as it can bring a fall in (his/her) life. I thank You, Lord, that Your Word is living and powerful, and sharper than any two-edged sword, piercing even to the division of _____ 's soul and spirit, (his/her) joints and marrow, and Your Word is a discerner of _____ 's thoughts and intents of (his/her) heart. Lord, help _____ to enter into Your rest and to be hidden inside of You. I thank You, Lord, that through this promise of rest _____ learns to trust You more and more, in Jesus' name. Amen.

Be still ...
Journal as you pray.

_____
_____
_____
_____
_____
_____
_____
_____
_____
_____
_____
_____
_____
_____
_____
_____
_____
_____
_____
_____
_____
_____
_____
_____
_____
_____
_____
_____
_____

"Rest"

Greek translation:
"anapauo"

A cessation from toil,
a refreshment, an intermission.

Day Six

Matthew 11:28-30
"Come to Me, all you who labor and are heavy laden, and I will give you rest. Take My yoke upon you and learn from Me, for I am gentle and lowly in heart, and you will find rest for your souls. For My yoke is easy and My burden is light."

Knowledge:

When I read this particular passage of scripture I had mixed feelings arise out of my soul. First of all, thinking about wearing any "yoke" does not give me the mental picture of entering into rest! These two words in my mind *yoke* and *rest* are oxymorons. They don't go together, they don't mix, and yet the Lord uses them together to make His point of entering into His kind of rest.

The word *rest* in this particular verse in the Greek language is the word, *anapauo* and is pronounced (an-ap-ow-oh). In the *Strong's Concordance[1]*, it is reference #373 with the definition *ana, which means "up" and pauo, which means "to make to cease."* The word describes *"a cessation from toil, a refreshment, an intermission."*

I have such vivid memories of growing up in Choctaw County, Mississippi, way out in the country! We had a huge garden, and truck patches (these were just different names for very large gardens that were away from the house!), and even acres and acres of cornfields. I was never the kind of little girl that you would say was a 'tomboy.' On the contrary, I was very much a girlie girl! But no matter how old we were, or where we fell in the rank and file of children, whether we were male or female we were expected to work, inside the house, and outside the house!

I didn't mind the inside work very much. Cleaning, cooking and washing, were chores that came naturally to me. But since my sister, Paulette and I were the first and second born children, with two younger brothers, Tim and Heath to follow, we girls were expected to work like boys. My sister didn't have too much trouble with this expectation. She could drive the tractor, plant the fields, run the cultivator, and harvest the fields... but not me! I was a musician! I did not like getting my hands dirty, and the job of driving the tractor was already taken! Needless to say, this station in life never fit me very well. But I gave it my best shot.

I remember one spring day so well. It was like it was yesterday. I must have been nine or ten years old, as my brother who is four years younger than me was out in the garden along with me. Daddy wanted to plow the garden but the tractor was already being used in the fields. Daddy told us that did not present a problem. He would just hook up the mule to the one-bladed plow and he could plow the garden that way.

I would not say either my brother or I were very bright at this point as we walked right into his little trap with the question, "Daddy, we don't have a mule anymore. What you gonna use to pull the plow?" Well, that was all it took! My daddy broke out in a grin from ear to ear as he answered our innocent little question, "Why, I am going to use you two as the mule! I am going to hook you two up to the yoke and you can pull the plow down the rows for me."

First of all, being a girlie girl, I was horrified that I was re-placing a mule! My five year old brother thought this was wonderful! How fun to be the mule, he thought, until we actually were hooked up to the plow and had to pull it down the rows! Of course, you know this was not a plan that actually worked, as I not only was a 'sissy,' but a small little girl, and my five year old brother was no power horse for pulling either! But it was one of those adven-tures as children that you never forget!

I will never forget thinking to myself that this is impossi-ble; I can't do this; this thing hurts my neck and shoul-ders; and finally the tears that streamed down my face as I pulled and struggled to no avail. Once the tears began to fall my daddy let us out of the harness, and of course, set us free, but not without much humiliation for me, glee from my brother who never figured out it was not a game, and much belly laughter from my daddy!

Over the years I have thought of this scenario so many times, and now instead of crying, it makes me laugh too, but I will never forget how that thing felt on my shoulders and how convinced I was that I was not created to even try to do this type of work, much less accomplish it.

When I read those precious words in Matthew 28 where the Lord, Himself, is calling me (and you) to, *"Come to Me all you who labor and are heavy laden,"* my first thought is how can anyone resist that invitation? And yet, I know from my own experience how I have heard those words many times and still in my stupidity, or weakness, or who knows what would cause me to resist such a won-derful invitation, yet, I would continue to try and do cer-tain things on my own. How silly of us to continue to try and pull that silly plow like my little brother and me, struggling, and fussing and fighting, getting nowhere at all, when we could shed that cumbersome, painful yoke that does not fit, and come to Him when He calls us.

Ownership:

Lord, forgive me when You have called to me, and I have ignored Your voice. Forgive me for trying to do so many things wearing a yoke that does not fit me, and for trying to accomplish a job that I am not capable of accomplishing, apart from You. Lord, I come to You now and I thank You that You give me rest and I receive it. I will take Your yoke upon me because it fits me perfectly and it is easy. It is not too heavy for me; in fact, it is light, as You are carrying it while I walk along under You. Lord, I ask You to teach me and I will learn from You. Thank You, my Lord, for being gentle and lowly in heart, and I thank You that I find rest for my soul in You, in Jesus' name. Amen.

Action:

Lord, I bring to You _____. Your Word says that when _____ comes to You, when (he/she) labors and is heavy laden, that You will give _____ rest. I thank You, Lord, that _____ takes Your yoke upon (him/her) and _____ learns from You, for You are gentle and lowly in heart, and _____ will find rest for (his/her) soul. Thank You, Lord, that Your yoke is easy and Your burden is light for _____, in Jesus' name. Amen.

Be still ...

Here is a place for your thoughts as you pray while you are being still in His presence.

_____

_____

_____

_____

_____

_____

_____

_____

_____

_____

_____

_____

_____

_____

_____

_____

_____

_____

_____

_____

_____

_____

_____

_____

_____

_____

_____

_____

_____

_____

_____

_____

_____

Day Seven

Revelation 14:13
*Then I heard a voice from heaven saying to me, "Write:
'Blessed are the dead who die in the Lord from now on.'"
"Yes," says the Spirit, "that they may rest from their
labors, and their works follow them."*

Knowledge:
When I talk to different people about their favorite scriptures in the Bible or their favorite books in the Bible,
hardly anyone ever says the book of Revelation! And yet,
there are so many wonderful treasures for us of hope, healing, and restoration hidden within these pages. In Revelation 14:13, some would say it is too hard to understand,
and when I hear those types of responses I usually say
maybe the reader should try a different translation. Our
Father God has not hidden anything from us, but rather,
He has hidden many secrets and revelations for us! Oh, I
have always been so hungry after the things of God! I remember in my late teens being quite frustrated in my pursuits of His presence and many times even staying away
from particular books for fear I might not understand
them.

One thing I am certain of now, all the scriptures are written *for us,* and that all things are for our understanding,
insight, wisdom, strength, peace, etc. Sometimes the understanding comes in due season, and this is the "waiting
time" during which most of us set up preconceived no-
tions concerning certain topics, books of the Bible, verses,
etc. I believe we are in a season when the Holy Spirit
longs to reveal certain truths to us to help us move

forward in our walk with Him. For instance, let's take a look at the same scripture from the Message Bible.

Revelation 14:13
I heard a voice out of Heaven, "Write this: Blessed are those who die in the Master from now on; how blessed to die that way!"
"Yes," says the Spirit, "and blessed rest from their hard, hard work. None of what they've done is wasted; God blesses them for it all in the end." (MSG)

Does this help you understand this passage of scripture any better? Well, let's focus on the phrase, *"blessed rest."* Is this not what all of us are seeking? When we enter into rest, we would much prefer for that time to be blessed, am I right? Of course, we want everything we do, and everything we are to be blessed! So why not learn how to enter into God's kind of rest and in this glorious opportunity receive God's blessings, also?

Over the past few years, we have focused on this "Be Still" message from the Lord. I think it can be so easily misunderstood, or even misinterpreted as if to say that we are saying not to "do" anything anymore! Nothing could be further from the truth! We understand that faith without results does not lead to life; we understand that we simply cannot sit around with our hands folded, and expect "fairy dust" to fall upon us! The pursuit in which the Holy Spirit has led us these past months is one of a higher level. A level that cannot be perceived through the mental thought process without the element of the Spirit of God showing us the way through this earth realm and into the heavenly way of thinking and being, even while we are still here on this earth.

> *I will do as you tell me, Lord.*

Have I lost you yet? I pray that I have not, as I want to impart to you that it is in our very *doing* for the Lord, that we learn to not waste our efforts but to only *do as we are told.* Jesus told his disciples that *He only does what the Father does.* So with this thought in mind, think and meditate on this scripture in Revelation. Of course, literally it can be explained as when we physically die in our flesh bodies that as long as we are saved, born again, and one with Christ, then we can enter into rest, but I truly believe there is so much more to it than that.

Look at it like this. While we still are breathing in this earth suit we call a body, we can "die to ourselves" and be hidden in the Master from this time and on into the future, with an eternal arrow on the end of our lives. In this way of "dying to self" we can understand how blessed we are to have the choice to "die" this way! Then the Spirit of God joins in the conversation, *"Yes, and blessed rest from (your) hard, hard work,"* He says. So does this mean that we don't need to "do" anything else as long as we breathe on this earth? God forbid!

This is not an excuse to never do anything else for the kingdom of God. This is not an excuse to never volunteer again in children's or youth church, or usher, or help in the kitchen! This is not an excuse at all, but a medal given to those who finally have found the passageway through the maze of 'striving, flesh struggles, self-promotion, approval seeking,' which is the result of our much doing! That's so exhausting! But now we can enter into His *"blessed rest,"* which brings about "much accomplished" without the driving force of our pride-filled need/desire to be acknowledged or approved!

The last line is such a great confirmation, also, when it says, *"None of what they've done is wasted; God blesses them for it all in the end."*

So have you been like me? Driven for some right reasons, but mostly for all the wrong reasons, then you catch a glimpse of yourself in the looking glass of the Spirit of God and don't like what you see? Let us not feel guilty for all the flesh works we have done. Rather, know that even in our ignorance, or wrong motives in our much 'doing,' God promises us that none of that has been wasted, and that He blesses us for it all in the end!

Now the real questions arise. Do I truly understand and recognize my weakness in my 'doing' for self-promotion and recognition? Do I understand that in this higher place of entering into God's rest, I can do what He tells me to do, and rest in knowing that He is actually doing it through me? When He is the One doing it through me, then I can take no glory and no honor for it. But I can rest in it, knowing that He has blessed, and will continue to bless, my willingness to be used when 'He says,' and my willingness to 'wait upon the Lord,' when He says to wait.

So don't beat yourself up over anything done or not done in the past. It is finished and God will reward. Our daily opportunity now is to "die" to self, our own will, and our own need to be approved and have our ego stroked for what we can get done.

My greatest understanding now is to guard against the 'Wonder Woman mentality' of self-promotion, and having my pride lifted high over all my "great accomplishments" for the kingdom of God. I now see that He is not impressed with my busy-ness. He is only pleased when I come to Him when He calls, and I can "die" to my self-will and self-promotion flesh needs. In this I am blessed and even what I do then is blessed. Will you join me today in allowing the Lord to work through us whether to be about much 'doing,' or simply 'being' at His feet? You are welcomed; you are invited with an engraved invitation from the throne of God that says, "Won't you join Me and come into My presence?"

Ownership:

Lord, I hear a voice out of heaven telling me to write this down in this journal. I hear Your voice wooing me to learn how to "die to myself" and to live in You. I accept that You are blessing me as I live in You from now on; and I realize that I am blessed to "die to myself," this way! I thank You, Lord, that I have ears to hear the voice of the Spirit of God, and I hear You say through Your Word, *"Yes, and blessed rest from hard, hard work."* Thank You, my Lord and King, that I am blessed and I can enter into Your blessed rest from the hard, hard work of my flesh. Most of all, I thank You, Father, that none of what I've done is wasted; I thank You and receive Your blessings, for it all will be blessed in the end, in Jesus' name. Amen.

Action:

Lord, for _____ I hear the voice of Your Spirit out of heaven. I thank You that You are wooing _____ to learn how to "die to self" and You are teaching _____ to live for You.   I ask You, Lord, to give _____ ears to hear when You are speaking by Your Spirit and by Your Word.   Thank You, Lord, for blessing _____ with rest from hard, hard work. Thank You, my King, that _____ is blessed and can enter into Your blessed rest from any and all flesh works. Finally, Lord, I thank You, that none of what _____ has done is wasted but that You bless (him/her) for it all in the end, in Jesus' name. Amen.

Be still ...

As the Spirit has told us in the scripture for today, *"Write this!"* Will you write down and journal what the Lord says to you through your prayer time?

_____

_____

_____

_____

_____

_____

_____

_____

_____

_____

_____

_____

_____

_____

_____

_____

_____

_____

_____

_____

_____

_____

_____

_____

_____

_____

_____

_____

Psalm 132:14

This is My resting place forever; Here I will dwell, for I have desired it.

Day Eight

Psalm 132:14
This is My resting place forever; Here I will dwell, for I have desired it.

Knowledge:
Be still and rest. Simple words to say, but many times very hard to do. It's not that I can't make myself sit down. I can, so can you, but to make my mind and thoughts 'be still,' hmm… this is a whole new ballgame.

Yesterday, our son Harry III, was sitting with me in our TV room, which we all have unofficially designated as our family's resting place. It's not where we pray in the early morning but rather where we rest and play together at night. This is where we play scrabble, or dominos, watch a movie, or talk as a family. H III and I were sitting together, the television was on but neither of us was really watching it. I was doing a Sudoku® puzzle and he had his laptop open and was reading about taxes, the news, and world events. I noticed that he was reading out loud, not too loud, but nonetheless he was reading out loud.

This got my attention as in the early morning hours when I am reading my Bible, many times I read out loud even when I am alone because it helps me focus, comprehend, and not let my mind wander off "doing" other things while it is supposed to be here with me *being still.* I asked H III why did he read aloud and he said almost exactly the same thing. I felt that was the answer but I wondered if he actually knew why he was doing it. I should have known he knew why, as he is a thinker, a contemplator, brilliant in his own God-given way.

As we talked together, I noticed something about him that I guess I have known all his life but still I am amazed many times at the wonders and creations of the Lord. When H III talked about needing to read aloud to stay focused, there was absolutely no condemnation, feelings of guilt, or regret, or shame, or anything else negative! I have always said that even as frustrating as he was to rear as a child, because you could not persuade him to do anything with any method (reward, guilt, shame, blame, punishment, approval, or disapproval), even as hard as it was to 'deal' with him without any of these methods, if we could bottle and sell what it is that makes him so unique, we would be worth billions of dollars!

How freeing it would be to not be controlled by any of those methods I mentioned above: reward, guilt, shame, blame, punishment, approval or disapproval! It's hard to fathom a world without these action-controlling methods, and yet, here the Lord has entrusted H III into our hands without the help of any of the behavior-controlling tools!

As frustrated as he has made me as a parent, I have also greatly envied him, too, as I wish that none of the above listed behavior 'pressure points' affected me! I have spent most of my life getting over these behavior-modification methods! But H III has never had to deal with them at all! I can't remember one instance in his entire life where these outside forces have caused him to do anything. He doesn't get ruffled or flustered or allow himself to be manipulated to do things or even think any certain way. Oh how I wish I was like him! But then, I can be, and so can you! How is that possible?

H III found a place inside the Lord very early in his life, a place where he is at total peace and rest, a resting place in

Christ. Today's scripture in Psalms is the Lord talking about His resting place, where He will abide forever, and yet, we are to find our resting place in Him, and we are to abide within Him forever, also. H III has found this place; I am continuing to find this place, and you can too. Will you continue on with me as we enter God's kind of resting place?

> *The more I seek You, the more I find You*

Ownership:

Lord, I want to be Your resting place forever. I want You to say that within my heart You will rest and dwell, for You have desired to live within me. I make this same commitment to You. I want You to be my resting place forever; I want to dwell hidden within You, for I desire to live in You and You in me, in Jesus' name. Amen.

Action:

Lord, I thank You that _____ wants to be Your resting place forever. _____ wants You, Lord, to say that within (his/her) heart You will rest and dwell, for You, Lord, have desired to live within _____. I ask You, Father, to woo the heart of _____ to You. _____ wants You to be (his/her) resting place forever and I confess this in the name of Jesus. _____ wants to dwell hidden within You, Lord, for _____'s desire is to live in You and You in (him/her). I pray this in Jesus' name. Amen.

Will you continue on with me as we enter God's kind of resting place?

Be still ...

Enter into Father God's rest right now. Journal what you hear Him say.

_____

_____

_____

_____

_____

_____

_____

_____

_____

_____

_____

_____

_____

_____

_____

_____

_____

_____

_____

_____

_____

_____

_____

_____

_____

_____

_____

_____

_____

_____

Jehovah Nissi
"His banner over us is love."

Entering Rest

Day Nine

Isaiah 11:10
And in that day there shall be a Root of Jesse, Who shall stand as a banner to the people; For the Gentiles shall seek Him, And His resting place shall be glorious.

Knowledge:

The Root of Jesse prophesied here, came in the flesh as Jesus Christ through the womb of Mary. Jesus stands even now as a banner to the people. He is my covering. He is your covering. We, as those outside Israel, Gentiles, not born as Jews, we seek Him as our own, and we find Him. In Him we find our comfort; He is our deliverer, Savior… our Lord. Most of all, we seek Him to find our place of peace, and rest. Let Him come against the struggle of our souls and bring us into the glorious place of His rest. I am willing to enter rest. Will you enter His rest with me?

The day of His rest is here. Jesus Christ is the Root of Jesse, and He is standing as *Jehovah Nissi,* which means, *"His banner over us is love."* He is our banner, our covering. The pronouncement of who He is and who I am inside of Him is upon us. We must seek Him today and always. He is the most glorious resting place for us!

There are times in our lives when we are so busy that we can't even see what is right in front of us. Why? Because we are not looking! There are times in our lives when we are so busy we can't even hear the voice of the bridegroom calling us to rest in His glorious resting place. Why? Because we are not listening! The Bible makes plain in the book of Revelation that the things of God are for those who *'have ears to hear what the Spirit is saying...'.* (Revelation 2:11) Can you hear Him?

Let us not fall short of entering into the most amazing and precious gift the Lord *is giving* to us. Notice the verb in the last sentence, *is giving;* right now, this very moment, the Lord God Almighty is holding out His rest, His gift of rest, outstretched toward us. I run to Him now. Will you run with me to receive this amazing gift of His rest?

Ownership:

Jesus Christ, the Root of Jesse, I call upon You today as my own Savior and Lord. I choose to enter into Your rest that You have prepared for me. I know by Your Word that You stand today and always as *Jehovah Nissi, Your banner over me is love.* You are covering me with Your love and I receive it. Your banner held high over my head reads, *"Jesus Christ, Jehovah Nissi, to whom I (put your name here) belong."* Lord, today and always, I seek You. You are the most glorious resting place for me, in Your name, Jesus Christ. Amen.

Action:

Jesus Christ, the Root of Jesse, stands today and always as *Jehovah Nissi, His banner over* _____ *is love.* His covering over _____ is love. The banner held high over _____'s head reads, *"Jesus Christ, Jehovah Nissi, to whom* _____ *belongs."* I declare today that _____ seeks Jesus Christ today and always. He is the most glorious resting place for _____, in Jesus' name. Amen.

Be still ...

His banner over you is *love* ... journal your thoughts.

LOVE

Day Ten

I Peter 2:9
But you are a chosen generation, a royal priesthood, a holy nation, His own special people, that you may proclaim the praises of Him who called you out of darkness into His marvelous light ...

Knowledge:

God has chosen you! Just think about that for a moment. As you read this scripture in a prayer to Father God, first over yourself and then over someone else, just imagine how much He loves you. He chose you; He positioned you in royalty and priesthood. He calls you holy, because He is holy and you are hidden in Him. You are special and you have been given a great assignment to proclaim His praises! Why? Because He called you out of darkness into His marvelous light!

This is not a light that you have to "come up with." This is not a light that you have to go after, search for and hopefully find. This is not a light that requires you to flip the switch in your own ability in order to cause the light to shine! No! This is His marvelous light and you have been called into this light! The best part is, when you walk into the light, you walk out of the darkness! What better turn around position could any of us hope for than to come out of the dark and into the light? Talk about a spiritual U-Turn! We are not just called to do this, created by God's own hands, with His own design within us, to feel, to see, and to hear Him calling us, but we are given this ultimate choice of our own! You may stay in darkness if you so choose, or you can come out of darkness and into *"His marvelous light!"*

When we look at it in these terms it is not hard to see that only someone completely stupid would continue to stay in darkness when they have been given a royal invitation from the throne room of God to come out of darkness and into the light! Come into My presence, says the Lord!

You are Cordially Invited
To Come Out of Darkness
Into God's Marvelous Light!
When? Today
Where? In God's Presence
RSVP Required

The royal invitation has been issued to you. Do you send your acceptance or your regrets? The choice is simply yours, but don't ever say that you were not invited because the royal decree has been sent out for you! You have been declared by the Lord Himself that you are a chosen generation. You are a royal priesthood. You are a holy nation. You are God's own special person. Why has all this been said about you and done for you?

So that you may proclaim the praises of Him who called you out of darkness into His marvelous light!

Ownership:

Lord, I accept Your royal invitation to come out of darkness and into Your marvelous light. I accept all that You say about me and I will declare Your praises wherever I go, today and always. I know by Your Word that I am a chosen generation, a royal priesthood, a holy nation, and Your own special person. Because of who You say I am, I rejoice in You, and find my resting place of who I am. I no longer have to strive to prove anything to anybody because I rest in You and who You are, in Jesus' name. Amen.

Action:

Lord, I thank You that Your royal invitation has been sent out to _____. You have invited (him/her) to come out of darkness and into Your marvelous light. I pray that _____ will accept all that You say about (him/her) and will declare Your praises wherever (he/she) goes today and always. By Your Word, You say that _____ is a chosen generation, a royal priesthood, a holy nation, and Your own special person. Because of who You say _____ is, _____ will rejoice in You, and find (his/her) resting place of who (he/she) is. _____ no longer has to strive to prove anything to anybody because _____ rests in You and in who You are, in Jesus' name. Amen.

Be still ...

Enjoy His presence right now. You are not required to do anything or be anybody. Just be still and know that He is your God! Here is a place for your thoughts.

One of the benefits of being engrafted into God's family is His promise to make me a house!

"House"

Hebrew translation:
"bayit"

A house, household, family, clan; temple, building, home, dwelling; house of God.

Day Eleven

II Samuel 7:10-12
Moreover I will appoint a place for My people Israel, and will plant them, that they may dwell in a place of their own and move no more; nor shall the sons of wickedness oppress them anymore, as previously, since the time that I commanded judges to be over My people Israel, and have caused you to rest from all your enemies. Also, the Lord tells you that He will make you a house. When your days are fulfilled and you rest with your fathers, I will set up your seed after you, who will come from your body, and I will establish his kingdom.

Knowledge:

In the scripture above, God makes a promise to Israel, and I believe to all of us who choose Jesus Christ as our Lord. We are then adopted into His family as His own which includes all the benefits of living in His kingdom. One of those benefits is His promise to make me a house! When Jesus Christ is your Lord, God promises to make you a house! The word *house* in the ancient Hebrew is the word *bayit*. It is pronounced (by-yut), and is *Strong's Concordance*[1] #1004. The definition of this ancient word is, *house, household, family, clan; temple, building, home.* *Bayit* occurs approximately 2,000 times in the Old Testament text. *Bayit* may refer to a *dwelling* such as in the Book of Ruth 2:7, or refer to a *family* as it does in Genesis 7:1. It's also the word for the *temple, the house of God* at Jerusalem, in II Chronicles 7:16.

When God makes us a promise to build us a house, it is so much more than a mere structure. He is building for us

(His bride), the house, the very home of homes inside Him. Jesus Christ is our bridegroom gone before us to prepare a place, a house, a home to bring His bride, to spend eternity with Him! In John 14:1-3 Jesus says, *"Let not your heart be troubled; you believe in God, believe also in Me. In My Father's house are many mansions; if it were not so, I would have told you. I go to prepare a place for you. And if I go and prepare a place for you, I will come again and receive you to Myself; that where I am, there you may be also."*

Many years ago, when I was in college at Mississippi State University, the Lord sent me a wonderful Christian room-mate, Pam Williams. She and I prayed and studied our Bibles and memorized scripture for the entire four years we were in college together. One of our favorite passages was this entire 14th chapter in John. Decades later, and it has been decades, these first verses continue to ring in my spirit throughout most days! What a blessed promise of rest, hope, assurance and trust. The Lord Himself, my bridegroom is building me a house, a place of rest and comfort, security and safety. In Christ, I can dwell and rest. It is one of my main daily goals, 'to stay in peace and rest.' It is a daily guarding of my heart and mind to not allow the enemy to slip in with worries and stresses that get me off my path of rest and peace. God has made me a promise. I fully intend to walk in it throughout my earthly days and into eternity hand in hand with my bridegroom. Can you make the same statement and really mean it? You should… right now.

Ownership:

Lord, I like it when You start a verse with 'moreover' as both of those words so fully describe a huge part of Your character. You are truly 'more' and You are always 'over' and above in everything! Thank You, Father, that You have appointed a place for me, and You will plant me, that I may dwell in a place of my own and move no more, nor shall the sons of wickedness oppress me anymore, as previously, since the time You commanded judges to be over Israel, and You have caused me to rest from all my enemies. Also, You tell me through Your Word that You will make a house for me. When my days are fulfilled and I rest with my fathers, You will set up my seed after me, who will come from my body, and You, Lord, will establish my children's kingdom. Most of all, I thank You, Father, that what You promised to Your servant David, You have also promised me, through the engrafting in of my soul through Your Son, and my Savior, Jesus Christ. Amen.

Action:

Lord, You are truly more than enough in all things. Thank You, Father, that You have appointed a place for _____, and You will plant _____, that (he/she) may dwell in a place of (his/her) own and move no more, nor shall the sons of wickedness oppress _____ anymore, as previously, since the time You commanded judges to be over Israel, and You have caused _____ to rest from all (his/her) enemies. Also, You tell me through Your Word that You will make a house for _____. When _____'s days are fulfilled and (he/she) rests with (his/her) fathers, You will set up _____'s seed after (him/her), who will come from (his/her) body, and You, Lord, will establish _____'s children's kingdom. Most of all, I thank You, Father, that what You promised to Your servant David, You have also promised _____, through the engrafting in of _____'s soul through Your Son, and _____'s Savior, Jesus Christ. Amen.

Be still ...

A place for your prayer thoughts.

_____

_____

_____

_____

_____

_____

_____

_____

_____

_____

_____

_____

_____

_____

_____

_____

_____

_____

_____

_____

_____

_____

_____

_____

_____

_____

_____

_____

_____

_____

Day Twelve

Psalm 37:7-8
Rest in the Lord, and wait patiently for Him; Do not fret because of him who prospers in his way, because of the man who brings wicked schemes to pass. Cease from anger, and forsake wrath; Do not fret - it only causes harm.

Knowledge:

What a wonderful scripture to help us understand God's very best for us! The sentences above contain the "understood subject." Remember seventh grade English? So, what is understood? **You!** You rest in the Lord! It is not a request! It is a command! You rest in the Lord. Honestly, if I could impart that one single commandment from the Lord into my own head, heart, mind, emotions, and physical being, oh how wonderful life would be!!!! I could float around on a daily fantasy ride of wonder and delight!! Doesn't it sound just grand to hear the Lord say, "You! Hey, you! I want you to rest in Me!" What would your quick response be? It should be, "Absolutely Lord! I would love to!"

Then why don't we? Maybe we just don't understand that this is God's best for us. Maybe we have yet to comprehend that it is more than a request but rather a command from the very throne of God! A commandment that we consistently disobey over and over again! Okay, when we say it like that, then maybe we should re-examine it a little further and figure out just exactly how the Lord intends for us to carry out this oh, so wonderful command of His!

Let's read it from the Message Bible.
Psalm 37: 7-8
Quiet down before God, be prayerful before him. Don't bother with those who climb the ladder, who elbow their way to the top. Bridle your anger, trash your wrath, cool your pipes - it only makes things worse. (MSG)

The Amplified Bible actually says to, *"Be still and rest!"* Even more to the point, right? Be still, quiet down, rest! It kind of reminds me of what we would hear if we were in a kindergarten class, huh? So the Father is talking to us, His kids, trying to get our attention to do what is necessary to help us with our daily lives. Alright, let's zip our lips and sit down criss-cross-applesauce and be still before our Teacher. Maybe it would help us to live longer if we could cease from anger, forsake wrath, quiet down, be still, and rest. I know one thing for sure and for certain, the Lord is helping us, if we will listen and obey.

> *I will just be still and rest, waiting patiently for You, Lord.*

Ownership:

Thank You, Lord, that You have asked me to rest in You. I want to obey You, Lord, today and always. Help me to rest in You, and wait patiently for You. Lord, I make a commitment to not fret because of him who prospers in his way, because of the man who brings wicked schemes to pass. Lord, I commit to cease from anger, and I commit to forsake wrath. I declare that I will not fret as it only causes harm, in Jesus' name. Amen.

Action:

Lord, I thank You that You have asked _____ to rest in You. _____ will obey You, in Jesus' name I declare and decree it. Lord, please help _____ to rest in You, and to wait patiently for You. Lord, I pray for _____ to not fret because of him who prospers in his way, because of the man who brings wicked schemes to pass. Lord, help _____ to cease from anger, and to forsake wrath. In the name of Jesus I thank You for revealing to _____ that when (he/she) frets and gets angry, it only causes harm, in Jesus' name. Amen.

Be still ...

Relax and let the Lord bear your burdens and carry your load right now. Rest in His presence and enjoy the still-ness of His voice. Journal what He says to you. It's okay to write down your feelings, too. Only the Lord knows.

_____

_____

_____

_____

_____

_____

_____

_____

_____

_____

_____

_____

_____

_____

_____

_____

_____

_____

_____

_____

_____

_____

_____

_____

_____

_____

Entering Rest

Day Thirteen

Isaiah 30:15
For thus says the Lord God, the Holy One of Israel; "In returning and rest you shall be saved; In quietness and confidence shall be your strength."

Knowledge:

The Lord God has made a way. He has already stamped out a path through the underbrush of our lives so that we can simply walk in the path He has made for us to the rest, security, quietness and confidence we have already been given through Jesus Christ. There is more strength obtained in the stillness of His presence than will ever be found through the conquering of others with a raised sword.

I grew up in the backwoods of the hills of Choctaw County, Mississippi and when I was a little girl, I loved the serenity of the wooded areas. I would get my chores done as quickly as possible and steal away into the woods to be alone... I was searching for quiet, a place to think and meditate and just 'be.' I have looked for fifty years and I still search for those same quiet places. I know how desperately I need a place to think, to not have to be 'on' for anyone. I am finally finding my 'be still' place at the feet of the One who loves me more than anything and anybody else, my Savior, Jesus Christ, who does not need me to perform or be 'on' for Him. With the One who is the lover of my soul, I can be still and not have to 'do' anything. In Him, I have found a quietness and confidence that gives me the strength to finish this life's course.

Life can be a wilderness of underbrush, thickets, thorns, and briars. If we are not careful we can get all caught up fighting our way through the self-made and self-imposed 'stuff' that clouds our view, and catches our feet on the way to the path of rest. The Lord has promised us a place in Him, a rest, quietness and confidence where our strength can be renewed and refreshed, where we can be restored simply by our stillness and acceptance of who He is, not in what we are capable of doing. The wiser I become, which is a nice way of saying I am getting older (haha!), the more I look for ways to walk in His paths and not paths of my own making and doing. He is calling us to come to Him, return to Him, rest in Him.

As a little girl, I had to push through the thickets, thorns and underbrush to find my way to a quiet spot. Now there is no need to go straight into the woods through the thickets, briars, thorns, and underbrush of this present life. If we will only take a moment and 'be still' He will show us the way to His quiet spot, and we can find the path that our heavenly daddy, Abba Father, has made for us. Won't you return with me to His presence of rest, quietness, and confidence, and together we can find our strength in Him?

I find my strength in the stillness.

Ownership:

Lord, I accept what You have said in Your Word as my own today. You have told me that I can return and rest in You and I can be saved. In quietness and confidence I shall be strengthened in Your presence. Lord, You are mine, and I am Yours. I am saved through Your grace and mercy. In the same way, I receive rest, a quietness to settle over my spirit, soul, and body, and in You I am confidently strong, in Your mighty name, Jesus Christ. Amen.

Action:

Lord, I pray that _____ accepts what You have said in Your Word as (his/her) own today. You have told _____ through Your Word that (he/she) can return and rest in You and _____ can be saved. In quietness and confidence _____ shall be strengthened in Your presence. Lord, You are _____'s, and (he/she) is Yours. _____ is saved through Your grace and mercy. In the same way, _____ receives rest, a quietness to settle over _____'s spirit, soul, and body, and in You _____ is confidently strong, in Your name, Jesus Christ. Amen.

Be still ...

By being still, I pray the Lord shows you the way to return to Him, to rest in Him, to be quiet and confident in Him and to find your strength. Here's a place for your thoughts as you pray.

_____

_____

_____

_____

_____

_____

_____

_____

_____

_____

_____

_____

_____

_____

_____

_____

_____

_____

_____

_____

_____

_____

_____

_____

_____

_____

_____

Day Fourteen

I John 3:24
Now he who keeps His commandments abides in Him, and He in him. And by this we know that He abides in us, by the Spirit whom He has given us.

Knowledge:

So how does the above scripture have anything to do with rest? Because dwelling in the Lord and abiding in His presence are the only ways we can truly find any lasting rest that brings about good results for us. In learning to be still and abiding inside of His presence, we learn to keep His commandments. In the Message Bible, this reads even more explanatory to me. What do you think when you read it?

I John 3:24
... As we keep his commands, we live deeply and surely in him, and he lives in us. And this is how we experience his deep and abiding presence in us: by the Spirit he gave us. (MSG)

There is a definite parallel between keeping His commandments and abiding in His presence. Notice that the Message Bible uses the wording, *"As we keep His commands."* To me this infers that our living deeply and surely in Him is dependent upon keeping His commandments. It makes sense to think that if we expect the benefits of a relationship that we should also have to walk in line with that relationship. We want the Lord to meet our needs, but we want that to be in spite of the fact that we live any way we want without any accountability on our end! Oh, when I say it that way, it sounds so selfish and self-focused! Oh, my goodness! If this is not exactly the problem of the world we live in, and this does not exclude what we term the 'church' either! I think the old saying that would best describe our attitude toward our relationship with the Lord would be, "We'd like to have our cake and eat it too!"

We all know that this is not a possible working relationship in any realm. So why do we approach our mental and emotional realm with our Father God with, "Lord I want all You can give me, but don't ask me for any obedience in return!" You and I both know this does not work, not with people, family, friends, or the Lord. If we want the benefits of kingdom relationship and abiding in His presence and resting in Him, then we must evaluate what we are going to trust Him with, and how willing we are to lay down our self-will, our self-focus and our selfish motives.

Today's devotional is a little more 'in your face,' I know, but I don't apologize for it, as the Lord deserves more from all of us than we have been giving Him. He deserves all of us! In light of who we actually are, He does not get much in return when what He gets is us!! But that's what He wants; He wants us. He wants me, and He wants you. That's all He asks is for us to trust Him with our future, our present, and our past. I give Him my all. Will you? No one can ever really know the answer to this question, except you. The Lord knows my heart and He knows yours.

> *Lord, I determine in my heart to keep Your commands, and I give You all of me.*

Ownership:

Lord, forgive me when I don't do what You command me to do. I ask that You help me to walk in obedience to Your will. Lord, I will keep Your commandments and abide in You and You in me. And by this I know that You abide in me, by the Spirit whom You have given me, in Jesus' name. Amen.

Action:

Lord, I ask You to reveal Your desire to abide in _____. Lord, as You show Your face to _____ may (he/she) long to obey Your command-ments and to abide in You from this day forth. By this may _____ know that You abide in (him/her), by the Spirit whom You have given _____, in Jesus' name. Amen.

Be still ...

Look, listen, and obey. Don't be afraid to write in your journal what the Spirit of God is saying to you.

_____

_____

_____

_____

_____

_____

_____

_____

_____

_____

_____

_____

_____

_____

_____

_____

_____

_____

_____

_____

_____

_____

_____

_____

_____

_____

_____

_____

_____

_____

_____

Day Fifteen

Leviticus 26:6
I will give peace in the land, and you shall lie down, and none will make you afraid; I will rid the land of evil beasts, and the sword will not go through your land.

Knowledge:

What a wonderful promise from the Lord, to give us peace! The original word in Hebrew that is the word *peace* in the scripture above, is synonymous with the word *rest.* It comes from the word *shalom* which in the *Strong's Concordance[1]* is #7965. Its various translated meanings are *completeness, wholeness, peace, health, welfare, safety, soundness, tranquility, prosperity, perfectness, fullness, rest, and harmony; the absence of agitation or discord. Shalom* is from the root verb, *shalam,* which means *to be complete, perfect, and full.* Shalom means much more than the absence of war and conflict.

It is the depth of wholeness, completeness, that we can never accomplish, grasp, obtain, or enter by our own abilities. Shalom is the wholeness that the human race seeks, to fill the void of our very existence. I believe that this void, divinely designed within each and every one of us, can only be filled by the One who created it in the first place. I believe, the lover of our souls, created each human being with a void within our souls that can only be satisfied and filled to overflowing by the great designer of humanity. God has put within each one of us, a huge hole that only He can fill and satisfy. We may search our entire lives over this entire world, gaining and attaining things, people, fame and fortune and still never put a dent in filling the huge puzzle piece void of our souls' existence, until we finally come to the end of our human searching and turn to the one true God who is ever calling us toward Himself. He not only has what we need to be 'shalom,' complete, and whole, finished, as it were... but, and hear this with your spirit ears, He actually *is* the puzzle piece that fits within each one of us, completing, satisfying, ful-filling, perfecting, harmonizing, prospering, peace-giving, health-making, safety-zoning, and rest entering, that our individual souls long for continually!

All the way back to Leviticus, God is making promises to us of who we can be, how we can live, and of future com-pletion of our eternal beings. So what's the drawback? Why do we shrink back in fear and not fulfill this amaz-ing promise by our own choice to reject this awesome puz-zle piece gift of God, Himself? Well, I guess that is the real question each one of us should ask ourselves today! I run to those beckoning arms right now! Will you run with me to Him, the lover of your soul, the completer of the rest you long to enter? He is waiting for you. Come home to His arms.

Ownership:

Lord, I recognize through Your Word that from the beginning of time until today, You have given me a promise of peace and rest. Your Word says that You will give me peace, rest, tranquility, prosperity, completeness, wholeness, perfectness, harmony, and so much more! You promise to give it to me in this land in which I live right now! Your Word promises that I shall lie down, and none will make me afraid. Your Word promises that You will rid the land of evil beasts, and the sword will not go through my land. I thank You, my Lord and my King for Your promises. I accept these promises as my own, and I trust You to do what You say You will do. Thank You, my Father, that it is not my job to try and do Your job. My job, my work, my part is to believe You, to trust You, to obey You. I accept my part today. Lord, I believe. Help me when I don't. I confess to trust You today and always and I ask You to give me the supernatural strength to do so! I pray in Jesus' name. Amen.

Action:

Lord, thank You for Your Word concerning _____.
I confess that _____ will receive all Your Word promises (him/her). The Lord will give peace (and rest) to _____ in the land, and _____ shall lie down, and none will make (him/her) afraid; Lord, You will rid the land of evil beasts, and the sword will not go through _____'s land, in Jesus' name. Amen.

Be still ...

Today's scripture is a powerful promise from the Lord to you personally. Don't just read it and go about your daily routine without taking the time to meditate on this huge promise. Can you believe the Lord today for the fulfillment of this scripture in your life? Why not take the time to meditate, mull this over and over quietly, reading the verse until you really get it past your head into your heart? Now, ask yourself this question, "What is keeping me from believing the Word of the Lord for me personally?" Write down your answer. Then offer it to the Lord as a sacrifice today as you repent of what has stopped you in the past from truly believing Him.

_____

_____

_____

_____

_____

_____

_____

_____

_____

_____

_____

_____

_____

_____

_____

_____

_____

_____

Day Sixteen

Numbers 6:24-26
"The Lord bless you and keep you; The Lord make His face shine upon you, and be gracious to you; The Lord lift up His countenance upon you, and give you peace."

Knowledge:

Once again we read a scripture with the synonym *peace* for *rest*. What an incredible prayer to say over ourselves and those we love each and every day! In fact, when we read it as it was written in context, it is a priestly blessing that Moses heard from the Lord and was told to give to Aaron (Moses' brother) and his sons. The Lord said in verses 22 through 26:

And the Lord spoke to Moses, saying: "Speak to Aaron and his sons, saying, 'This is the way you shall bless the children of Israel. Say to them: "The Lord bless you and keep you; The Lord make His face shine upon you, and be gracious to you; The Lord lift up His countenance upon you, and give you peace."'"

These precious words are straight from the mouth of the Lord given on command to priests to bless the people. The Bible tells us in the New Testament that when we receive Jesus Christ as our Lord and Savior, we are then elevated in rank position to priesthood.

I Peter 2:9
But you are a chosen generation, a royal priesthood, a holy nation, His own special people, that you may proclaim the praises of Him who called you out of darkness into His marvelous light ...

We should not only be receiving this blessing daily into our own personal lives and walks with the Lord, but we should be proclaiming this to each other! From the moment we rise, we should be blessing our husbands, wives, children, mothers, fathers, sisters, brothers, co-workers, friends and neighbors with this proclamation from the Lord!

"Hey, neighbor! The Lord bless you and keep you; The Lord make His face shine upon you, and be gracious to you; The Lord lift up His countenance upon you and give you peace." They might give you a funny look but you might be surprised! You might be the very words of love, encouragement and blessing that their hearts were crying out for only moments before! Why not go ahead and fulfill your priesthood position through your own words today? What do you have to lose? Absolutely nothing! I proclaim over the very one who is reading this right now, as you hold this book in your hands, and your mind is reading these simple words, hear this!

> "I bless you today and I ask the Lord to bless you and keep you throughout this entire day; I ask the Lord to make His face shine upon you, and be gracious to you; I ask the Lord to lift up His countenance upon you and give you peace! Shalom!"

The silly little southern girl in me always wants to say, "Shalom, ya'll," with a big ol' drawl! Try it, you might actually make yourself smile today!

So here is the challenge today: First, receive and respond to God's blessing to you, over you, and through you. Second, understand that it is given to you, not only to accept as your own, but then for the Lord to be able to use your mouth as His own priest's mouth to proclaim praises and blessings upon His people wherever you go today and always.

So get ready to speak this prayer out loud over yourself and over others throughout today. Ready... set... go!!!!! Go bless somebody today.

> *Today, I will speak blessings upon the people in my life!*

Ownership:

Lord, I hear Your words to my heart today and I choose to receive Your blessings in my life. I accept that You are blessing me and keeping me. I accept that You are making Your face to shine upon me, and You are being gracious to me! Lord, thank You for Your grace! I need it so much! I accept that You, Lord, are lifting up Your countenance upon me and giving me the peace and rest, the shalom, for which my heart, mind, and daily life longs! I accept Your blessing of shalom today and always, in Jesus' name. Amen.

Action:

Lord, today I pray for _____. I bless _____ with Your commanded words that I am to speak over (him/her) today. May the Lord bless _____ and keep _____; may the Lord make His face to shine upon _____, and be gracious to _____; may the Lord lift up His countenance upon _____ and give (him/her) peace and rest. I speak shalom to _____ in Jesus' name. Amen.

Be still ...

Can you receive the blessing of the Lord today? He is giving it; now it is up to you to simply receive it! Listen and learn of Him, for He cares for you!

_____

_____

_____

_____

_____

_____

_____

_____

_____

_____

_____

_____

_____

_____

_____

_____

_____

_____

_____

_____

_____

_____

_____

_____

_____

_____

_____

_____

Day Seventeen

Luke 10:38-42

Now it happened as they went that He entered a certain village; and a certain woman named Martha welcomed Him into her house. And she had a sister called Mary, who also sat at Jesus' feet and heard His word. But Martha was distracted with much serving, and she approached Him and said, "Lord, do You not care that my sister has left me to serve alone? Therefore tell her to help me." And Jesus answered and said to her, "Martha, Martha, you are worried and troubled about many things. But one thing is needed, and Mary has chosen that good part, which will not be taken away from her."

Knowledge:

I am a southern reared lady from the great state of Mississippi. We southern ladies have always taken great satisfaction (that's a nicer sounding word for pride) in our hospitality skills. In fact, the motto for Mississippi is, "The Hospitality State." My mother is a great hostess, a wonderful cook, and a servant to everyone who comes to her home, or her church. I am a lot like my mother in many ways.

Over the past few years, the Lord has been dealing with me over those things that drive us to 'be the way we are.' He has been dealing with me so strongly, even to the point that last year, He commanded us to come off the traveling evangelistic road after thirty years and "be still!" I cannot say that it was an easy period of time. Hardly! For months, the Lord would not allow us to go out at all, and for me, who has much of my own personal identity based in what

I do, this has been one of the harder times in my personal growth time in the Lord.

I have adjusted to it and have accepted it as training, and can now tell about it, teach what I have learned to others, and hopefully, never have to go through it again. The impartation that I want to share with you may take the remainder of this book, but I believe the Lord will help me get this heart preparation message to you.

I have become Martha. My sister, Paulette, who is five years older than me, tells me that I was not always Martha. She says that when we were younger, she was the one left serving and I was Mary sitting at Jesus' feet! Maybe I was Mary when I was younger, but many 'people-pleasing/approval-driven' years have caused me to step over into Martha to the point that I no longer even remember the Mary in me!

As the Lord has continued to say to me, "Be still," these past many months, I am having to face many unflattering facts about myself. But in the facing and admitting to myself these very sobering, environmental personality traits that I have attained, and quite possibly, have become, I now realize that only with the help of my Lord, Jesus Christ, can I ever get back to where the Lord created me within the scope of who I really am.

In this story we can see a few things. First of all, Martha is most probably the older sister, as the Bible refers to the house as 'her house.' So Martha was inviting Jesus to come to her house and her sister Mary was living with her. Mary was most probably the younger sister, being reared by Martha.

When Jesus came into the house, Mary made a beeline to His feet which we see was obviously pleasing to the Lord. Mary came to listen, to hear, and to learn from Him. And here are the clincher words for all of eternity for some of us if we don't get over ourselves. *"But Martha was distracted ..."* Oh, how I do not want to get to heaven and hear these words as I stand before the Father God, "But Cheryl, you were distracted!" And yet, for many of us, if we do not change the way we are, or the way we have become, these are most probably the words we will hear! Lord, forgive me, and help me! I want to be able to sit at Your feet without the distractions of the world around me!

Jesus never scolded Martha for what she was doing. Her 'works' were not the problem. She was preparing a meal and that was fine. But what Jesus did tell her rings in my ears regularly now. And when I hear the Lord's voice and He says my name twice like Jesus said Martha's name, oh, how I am certain I have slipped back into my old 'doing' ways. *"Martha, Martha, you are worried and troubled about many things..."* Have you been worried and troubled about many things, and not allowed yourself to yield to His gentle urging to run to Him and sit at His feet?

"Martha, Martha, you are worried and troubled about many things, but one thing is needed ..." One thing is needed. The type A personality of Martha must have freaked out over those words! She must have been saying to herself, "You mean in all that I am doing, I have missed something? I forgot one thing! What did I forget?"

"Martha, Mary has chosen that good part, which will not be taken away from her." And without having to say it out loud Martha heard, *"...and Martha, you have not made that good choice."* What a blow to the ego and pride

of the one who 'always took care of everything.'

Martha must have been reeling inside trying to figure out where she fit, and where she belonged! She had spent so many years fulfilling the 'mother' role in her home that somewhere along the line, she forgot how to sit at the feet of Jesus.

Don't get me wrong. Somebody has to prepare the meal, and somebody has to be the mama in the house. These are obvious things that must be done, and this role needs to be filled. There is nothing wrong with the role of the mother or woman of the house. We all thank God for those who prepare meals, cook, clean, organize and keep the family in order and on time. Somebody's got to do this!

I am not minimizing this role at all, nor am I scolding you or me for fulfilling it. What I am saying is when my identity is more based on what I do rather than who I am, and when I have learned to be identified more with doing than with being, then I have lost my way to His feet and I need to get back to His way of being.

So the question still remains, "Which one are you? Martha? Mary?"

Only you can answer for sure, because the identification is not even made as much in what you do, but more in who you are, or who you are not in your heart of hearts.

> *I will not be so distracted (like Martha), that I fail to choose the 'good part.' Mary chose the good part.*

Ownership:

Lord, I want to be Mary sitting at Your feet. I want to be the one who, without even one thought or contemplation, chooses to sit down with You, before heading to the kitchen. I know You have put within me the heart to want to serve others, also, and I thank You for this wonderful gift. I choose to serve You as I serve others, but when the choice is set before me to run to the kitchen to be distracted by much doing, rather than to be still and sit at Your feet and learn from You, help me, Lord, to make the right choice. I want the better thing, the good part, the one thing that is needed, the only thing that matters. I want You. I choose You. Everything else is details, in Jesus' name. Amen.

Action:

Lord, I ask You to help _____ learn how to simply sit at Your feet. Lord, when the choice is given to be with You, to learn from You, to listen to You, or run around doing many distracting things, help _____ to be able to discern between the two choices and make the better one. Lord, thank You that _____ is a servant, and loves to help all those around (him/her). Thank You, that _____ loves to serve You. Lord I thank You, that just as You are teaching me the value of being still at Your feet, I also thank You that You are teaching _____ to be still and rest at Your feet. _____ will choose You, and remember that everything else is details in (his/her) life, in Jesus' name. Amen.

Be still ...

Don't be afraid to sit still at the feet of Jesus. There is no need for an agenda, a list, or even mental thoughts of what you need to say or do. For the moment, just relax and be still. During your prayer time, try listening instead of talking. Be still and journal what you hear Him say to you.

_____

_____

_____

_____

_____

_____

_____

_____

_____

_____

_____

_____

_____

_____

_____

_____

_____

_____

_____

_____

_____

_____

_____

_____

_____

Day Eighteen

Luke 10:38-42

Now it happened as they went that He entered a certain village; and a certain woman named Martha welcomed Him into her house. And she had a sister called Mary, who also sat at Jesus' feet and heard His word. But Martha was distracted with much serving, and she approached Him and said, "Lord, do You not care that my sister has left me to serve alone? Therefore tell her to help me." And Jesus answered and said to her, "Martha, Martha, you are worried and troubled about many things. But one thing is needed, and Mary has chosen that good part, which will not be taken away from her."

Knowledge:

I know we used this same scripture yesterday but there is too much in here to miss. If we don't get the full revelation of this wonderful scenario, it may be harder to enter into the full rest the Lord has made available for us. Martha was not hesitant to welcome Jesus into her home. Martha was a wonderful lady; it's obvious that her desire to have Jesus in her home was genuine. But like many of us, Martha's heart may have been right, but she was distracted by what she felt she needed to do. Quite possibly she was scrutinized by other women in her life, or neighbors, or family. Maybe she made regular choices, not based upon her own convictions as much as based upon pleasing others, or even simply upon what was expected of her?

Martha invited Jesus to her home and her desire was to make Him feel welcome and to prepare a meal for Him. I wonder when Jesus said to her that she was troubled about many things, but only one thing was needed ... could He have been speaking so literally to mean that Martha was preparing many different dishes for the meal, when all He needed was something simple, and less time-consuming? What if He was saying to her that He came to her house not for her to prepare a meal for Him, but could Jesus have been saying, "Martha, I came here today to prepare a table for you in the presence of your enemies."? (Psalm 23:5)

The people we find ourselves living to please are not enemies in our natural lives, but it is quite possible that they are enemies to our eternal spiritual peace and rest. When we are expected by others, or even struggling under self-imposed expectations, we can lose sight of what is true, and real and worthwhile. I believe Jesus was saying to Martha, "While you have received Me into your home, Mary has received Me into her heart."

We type A's (I am a recovering type A) can get so busy doing, doing, doing that we don't even realize that our doing many times is nothing more than a smokescreen to try and hide, or camouflage our lack of being still at His feet! And we type A's are not happy when we are just busy, busy, busy! Oh no, our busy-ness is not nearly enough to satisfy this driving force of energy! We type A's are not simply happy when we are allowed to do for others. We are not happy until everyone around us is as busy as we are!

That's why we see Martha boldly approaching Jesus without any thought that He might reprimand her in her own choices. Why would this not occur to Martha? Because we who find our complete identity in what we 'do, do, do,' even when we do what we do for the Lord, we find our identity in our busy-ness and we have no clue how to simply be identified with our 'being,' with who we are as a human being!

I find it interesting that when the Lord made all of us, He called us human beings, not human doings! But many of us have spent a lifetime more comfortable in our 'doing... what we do,' than our 'being... who we are.' Mary was comfortable in her being and quite possibly was finding that her own being was not satisfying or filling the void she had found in her life. Maybe she saw Jesus as He came into her home, and it was the pull of the fulfillment of her identity - to be identified with Christ. For throughout my years of studying the Bible, I can't find one single passage that supports *what we do* in place of *who we are!* We are to be saved, not 'do saved.' We are to be reconciled to God, not 'do reconciled.' We are to be one with Christ, not 'do one with Christ.' We are to be sanctified, be holy, be righteous, not 'do' any of these things.

Please do not misunderstand what I am saying. I am not saying that we are not to do anything. Nothing could be further from the truth! The Bible is clear, and our own hearts long to do for others. We are to love one another, to help one another, to serve, and be served. There is so much to do! Jesus even said to His parents when He was about twelve years old that they should not have been surprised when they lost Him for two days as He had to be about His Father's business; and He was not talking about carpentry work or His earthly father, Joseph.

This revelation on 'being versus doing' is not an excuse for the lazy Christian to do nothing. Most of those people are already easily identified, as they do nothing already. They are always the ones who just can't get up in the morning. They usually can't seem to go to bed either, as they find much place in the night for their lazy attitudes and actions to stay hidden from the accountable eye of others.

I am speaking to the hearts of those who long to be identified with Christ, but have found themselves *doing, doing, doing* to hide their lack of *being.* Our hearts cry out to our Savior, "Help me learn to be still and to be comfortable enough to sit at Your feet, Lord!"

When I read what Martha said to Jesus, *"Do You not care that my sister has left me to serve alone?"* my heart breaks for her. Why? Because I see myself many times over the years saying those very words to the Lord about others as I labored and struggled, toiled, worried and troubled myself about much 'doing.' So many times we have all wanted to scream at the Lord and say just as Martha did, "Make my sister help me, Lord!"

Jesus did not say all that Martha had done was wrong. He did not say that what Mary chose was right. He simply said that Mary had chosen that good part which will not be taken away from her. When the Lord gives us a portion of Himself at His feet, no one can take Him from us. My heart cries to recognize the distractions for what they are, and for the Lord to help me make better choices about where I spend my time, money, efforts, and energy. I feel Him calling me now to His feet. Won't you join me? Look for me… I'll be the one flat on my face worshiping Him.

Ownership:

Lord, please forgive me when I am too busy to even notice Your beckoning me to Your feet. Forgive me when I actually see and hear You, but choose to ignore You, for what others might think I need to be 'doing.' Lord, I choose to serve You, worship You, and do this as You command. Right now, I hear Your Word saying for me to 'be still.' I choose to sit at Your feet like Mary who has chosen the better part which cannot be taken away from her. I want to choose to sit at Your feet and receive that better part of You, that cannot be taken away from me either, in Jesus' name. Amen.

Action:

Lord, I pray for _____ today. I ask You to forgive _____ when (he/she) gets too busy to notice or hear You when You call. Lord, please show _____ how to relax and enjoy the journey of relationship with You. _____ longs to serve You, to worship You, to do those things that need to be done for Your kingdom, Lord. But Father, I ask that You teach _____ how to slow down, enter into Your rest, and learn to be still when You say. Lord, I declare that _____ chooses to receive that better part of You that cannot be taken away from (him/her), in Jesus' name. Amen.

Be still ...

Breathe deeply of His presence without having to hear or see. *Feel Him around you ... with you.* Be with Him now. Don't even try and write it down yet. Later on when you feel Him say that you can, take the time to write it all down. Don't worry how you write, or what you write. This is your journal, your love diary between you and the very lover of your soul, Jesus Christ. He is your bridegroom. Tell Him how much you love Him and long for Him.

_____

_____

_____

_____

_____

_____

_____

_____

_____

_____

_____

_____

_____

_____

_____

_____

_____

_____

_____

_____

_____

_____

_____

_____

Day Nineteen

John 6:26-29
Jesus answered them and said, "Most assuredly, I say to you, you seek Me, not because you saw the signs, but because you ate of the loaves and were filled. Do not labor for the food which perishes, but for the food which endures to everlasting life, which the Son of Man will give you, because God the Father has set His seal on Him."
Then they said to Him, "What shall we do, that we may work the works of God?"
Jesus answered and said to them, "This is the work of God, that you believe in Him whom He sent."

Knowledge:

My search for understanding and revelation is in how to balance our need to be still and learn of Him, with our need to do the things necessary for the kingdom to be finished, for the bride to be made ready, and for my own life to be ready to meet Him in the air at the trumpet sound! Although my natural personality has always prompted me to 'do,' as I grow in wisdom with the Lord, I can't just ignore those parts of my being that are not as natural as the other parts! Doing is more natural for me, but the Lord said that I am to 'die to myself and live for Christ.' This means I can't simply do the easier parts and pretend the other pull to 'be still' is not even there! I can't do this and neither can you!

Just help me find the balance, Lord.

Maybe that is why this passage of scripture in John has turned out to be such a huge help to me in understanding the depths and heights of this revelation of entering into

God's rest, and yet, not sitting on the sideline! In this particular story, Jesus has fed thousands of people, then sent the disciples ahead of Him in the boat. He then decides to join them and does so by walking across the Sea of Galilee on foot! He feeds the people then He walks on water! Wow! I guess we don't see that every day! Once He finds Himself on the other side with His disciples, these certain men find Him, join Him and begin to ask Him questions. These men want to know how to *'work the works of God.'*

Oh, what a huge question! Is this not the simplistic version of what many of us spend years praying to the Father? "Lord, show me what I am to do! Lord, show me how to do it! Lord, give me direction to my destiny!" On and on the questions are prayed, and the answers are sought year after year, decade after decade, generation after generation. And yet, here is the question and the answer all boiled down and made very simple.

Jesus told them to not labor for the food which perishes. Was Jesus saying that we are not to work? Of course not. The Bible also says a *"...laborer is worthy of his hire."* (I Timothy 5:18b, AMP) The Bible says, *"A little sleep, a little slumber, a little folding of the hands to sleep - so shall your poverty come upon you like a prowler, and your need like an armed man."* (Proverbs 6:10-11) It is obvious that Jesus is not telling these men to not work or to not labor. But He is about to tell them that the works of the kingdom can't be measured with the same measuring stick we measure earthly works.

I believe Jesus is saying that we are not to labor only for the food that perishes, but we are to labor, also, for the food which endures to everlasting life. Jesus goes on to say that this food which endures to everlasting life is what the Son of Man will give us! Are you completely confused yet? Don't be! It is quite simple really. Every day we all go about our daily routine, doing what is necessary to take care of our homes, family, children, marriages, etc. These are necessary things to do, but should never be so all-consuming that we don't remember to take care of those eternal things that will last forever!

The best part for me is the simple answer given to the direct question by the men. So the men ask, *"What shall we do? What shall we do? What shall we do, that we may work the works of God? What shall we do to 'work the works' of God?"* Now just stop and think about this! Am I God? Are you God? So what can you possibly do to work the works of God???? You can do nothing! You are not capable of working the works of God in the sense that we think of the word 'work!' Ah, but Jesus does not hit them upside the head and say, "Duhhhhhhhh ..." does He?

No. He answers them with the most profound answer for the universe. Jesus Christ, Messiah and King of Kings, actually tells these men how to work the works of God. Jesus Christ answers the universal question of, "What am I to do?"

I believe Jesus lowered His chin, and looked them straight in the eyes. I believe He paused long enough that all the men realized the answer to the longing of the soul was about to be spoken. As He opened His mouth, these words came forth, *"This is the work of God, that you believe…"*. **The work of God is that we believe!** Oh, don't get deflated and say to yourself, "Oh, that … *believe.* I am already doing that!" Don't kid yourself. We are not working the works of God. We are not believing. Believing as we are commanded to do requires everything within us all day, every day, focusing on Him only, wrestling our own minds, wills, and emotions to the ground through each and every day and even into the night.

We are required to believe in Jesus Christ whom God Himself sent! **Believe.** This is our work, and it is hard work, coming against our own ways of being trained in this natural realm. Believe that He is able. *"Simply believe,"* Jesus said to Jairus as his daughter lay literally dead on her bed. Simply believe. (Luke 8:50)

It is not a hard task but it is an all-consuming lifetime commitment to grow and go past where we are at this moment. It is a lifetime commitment to die to ourselves and live for Him. Most of us can talk the talk in our generation but how about walking it out, daily believing Him for everything and anything? Today is a good day to start believing that He is. Believe that He is God. Believe that He is able. Believe that He can help you enter into His rest that has been given to you.

Ownership:

Jesus, I commit to You today that I will not simply labor for food which perishes, but I will choose to labor for the food which endures to everlasting life. I believe that You give this to me because God the Father has set His seal upon You. Lord, I commit to hear You when You tell me how to work the works of the kingdom of God. I hear You tell me now to simply believe. I choose to believe You, my Lord. I believe. Help my unbelief, in Jesus' name. Amen.

Action:

Jesus, I commit _____ to You today. I ask You to be with (him/her) and teach _____ not to simply labor for natural food which perishes, but to choose to labor for the food which endures to everlasting life. _____ will believe that You give this to (him/her) because You are the Son of God, and Father God has set His seal upon You. Lord, I ask You to help _____ hear You when You tell (him/her) how to work the works of the kingdom of God. I hear You tell _____ now to simply believe. I declare by Your Word that _____ chooses to believe You, Lord. Help (his/her) unbelief, in Jesus' name. Amen.

Be still ...

Let's all get over ourselves today and lay our lives at His feet. Ask Him to help you believe more, and doubt less. Ask Him to help you identify those things, places, events, thoughts, whatever it is that is keeping you from a deeper and more intimate way of living and believing Him fully. Don't be afraid to write it down as it comes to you. Deal with it. Admit it and quit it, okay?

_____

_____

_____

_____

_____

_____

_____

_____

_____

_____

_____

_____

_____

_____

_____

_____

_____

_____

_____

_____

_____

_____

_____

_____

Luke 8:50

"Simply believe."

Day Twenty

John 12:1-8

Then, six days before the Passover, Jesus came to Bethany, where Lazarus was who had been dead, whom He had raised from the dead. There they made Him a supper; and Martha served, but Lazarus was one of those who sat at the table with Him. Then Mary took a pound of very costly oil of spikenard, anointed the feet of Jesus, and wiped His feet with her hair. And the house was filled with the fragrance of the oil. But one of His disciples, Judas Iscariot, Simon's son, who would betray Him, said, "Why was this fragrant oil not sold for three hundred denarii and given to the poor?" This he said, not that he cared for the poor, but because he was a thief, and had the money box; and he used to take what was put in it. But Jesus said, "Let her alone; she has kept this for the day of My burial. For the poor you have with you always, but Me you do not have always."

Knowledge:

Martha served the meal. Lazarus ate at the table with the others. And where was Mary? Was she helping Martha in the kitchen or with the serving at the table? No, Mary ran to get her most precious possession, the most valuable gift she owned had to be brought to Him! I can just see the younger sister now as Martha was busy, busy, busy, still trying to figure out what in the world Jesus could have been talking about when He had told her to choose the better part. Where was Mary? She was digging under all the many things in her storage closet, most probably under the pile of her belongings, to finally feel the beautiful oil and its container in her hands.

She did not make a big show of what she was about to do. She did not have to announce what she felt in her heart she must do. Why, I am fairly certain that once she got that bottle of oil in her hands the tears began to fall down her cheeks as her head began to grasp what her heart already knew. The King of Kings was gently calling her, Spirit to spirit, to bring the oil and prepare the awesome King of Glory for His upcoming death and burial. Have you ever done these types of things? You hear His voice, and you begin to obey, realizing in your head what it is you have said yes to, long after your heart has agreed!

Mary did not even slow her pace. I don't believe she even made a sound. I don't believe the others at the table even noticed her. But Jesus knew. He saw her coming, and with those eyes that bypass your earth suit and look through your flesh to the very core and essence of your being, of who you and I really are, He saw her. I can just imagine a gentle smile spreading across His lips, not for what she was about to do, not because His feet were about to be anointed. I imagine Him smiling because she simply obeyed His voice, and believed in her heart. Mary knew Him. Jesus knew her with an intimacy that could not be taken from her ... ever.

When we obey the calling of the Lord, some people will misunderstand our motives. Others will criticize or condemn us. Some will call us names, like foolish, childish, silly, or as Judas did, wasteful! Jesus quieted them all with the profound words that set the record straight. These are not the actual words recorded but I can just hear Jesus saying, "Out of all of you in this room, Mary is the one who knows Me. She knows who I am, and where I am going. She is foretelling by her actions My upcoming death and burial, and while I am still here she is showing Me how much she loves and cares for Me."

No one else did a thing for Him that day, not really. Oh, Martha may have fed his earthly stomach, but Mary fulfilled His eternal longing for His bride. For a few moments, Mary foretold her love for Him throughout eternity. Will you sit at His feet today? You don't need to bathe His feet or anoint His feet but you most certainly can love Him, at His feet.

> *Get on your knees; fall on your face; worship Him!*

Ownership:

Lord, I commit to come to Your feet to worship You, to love You, and to be with You. Forgive me, Lord, when I choose so many other things to 'do' instead of choosing to 'be' with You. Help me to know and understand those eternal lasting things as Mary did. Help me to overcome my people-pleasing desire to do when my doing is only a smokescreen to try and hide who I am not being. Lord, I want to be saved, to be filled with Your Holy Spirit, to be holy as You are holy, to be righteous through Your righteousness, and so much more. I long to simply be with You. Lord, I worship You today in spirit and in truth. I ask You to help me see myself as I really am, without the rose-colored glasses I wear to try and hide my selfish and self-focused self. Lord, I want to be all about You, and not about me. Forgive me when I have failed to see You as You really are, my Lord, and my King, in Jesus' name. Amen.

Action:

Lord, I commit _____ to You today and I ask that You draw (him/her) to Your feet to worship You, to love You, and to be with You. I ask You to forgive _____ when (he/she) chooses so many other things to do instead of choosing to be with You. Lord, please help _____ to know and understand those eternal lasting things as Mary did. Please help _____ to overcome people-pleasing desires to do when (his/her) doing is only a smokescreen to try and hide who (he/she) is not being. Lord, I ask that You show _____ the truth that only in being saved, filled with Your Holy Spirit, holy, righteous, and so many more traits of who You have called and created us to be that _____ will find the rest that (he/she) longs for. Lord, draw _____ to Your feet to be all about You, and not about (himself/herself). I ask You, my Father, to forgive _____ when (he/she) fails to see You as You really are, Lord and King, in Jesus' name. Amen.

Be still ...

There is no place quieter than at His feet. At the feet of our Lord and Savior there is only the sound of His voice. So listen, be still and quiet. Come with me and let's enter into His rest today. It's a journey, not just a destination. Let's enjoy each day, each step, each turn. He is calling you; won't you come?

_____

_____

_____

_____

_____

_____

_____

_____

_____

_____

_____

_____

_____

_____

_____

_____

_____

_____

_____

_____

_____

_____

_____

_____

Day Twenty-One

Matthew 6:25-34

(Jesus is speaking) *"Therefore I say to you, do not worry about your life, what you will eat or what you will drink; nor about your body, what you will put on. Is not life more than food and the body more than clothing?*

"Look at the birds of the air, for they neither sow nor reap nor gather into barns; yet your heavenly Father feeds them. Are you not of more value than they?

"Which of you by worrying can add one cubit to his stature?

"So why do you worry about clothing? Consider the lilies of the field, how they grow: they neither toil nor spin;

"and yet I say to you that even Solomon in all his glory was not arrayed like one of these.

"Now if God so clothes the grass of the field, which today is, and tomorrow is thrown into the oven, will He not much more clothe you, O you of little faith?

"Therefore do not worry, saying, 'What shall we eat?' or 'What shall we drink?' or 'What shall we wear?'

"For after all these things the Gentiles seek. For your heavenly Father knows that you need all these things.

"But seek first the kingdom of God and His righteousness, and all these things shall be added to you.

"Therefore do not worry about tomorrow, for tomorrow will worry about its own things. Sufficient for the day is its own trouble."

Knowledge:

Entering into God's rest is the goal, the prize, the destiny! There is no doubt we must keep our eyes on the prize and run the race to win! These are absolutes. We have established that to enter into the rest the Lord has promised us, according to Hebrews 4, many of us will need to labor, focus and work hard at entering rest. But that's not all we need to do to enter into this promised position and destiny of rest. Many of us have been like runners in a race, trying to run to the finish line with heavy weights tied around our ankles.

One of these heavy weights around our flesh bodies is worry. Worrying cannot add one thing to our being. The Bible says so plainly in today's scripture, *"Which of you by worrying can add one cubit to his stature?"* And yet so many people who say they love God, and that Jesus is their Lord go through this earth life trying to attain the promise set before them, while continuing to hold on to the self-imposed weights of worrying and fretting as if they were the badges of honor for their very lives' existence.

Worrying and fretting is very simple. It's sin. Oh, yes it is; it is disobeying the very words of Jesus. But many Christians still do it day in and day out! Why would we entertain such horrible daily traits and welcome them into our personalities? Because by worrying and fretting over anything and everything we are still in control. We who continue to worry and fret, even after we see plainly that it is sin, are holding on to control instead of learning to cast every care upon the Lord, for He cares for us.

When we worry, we are saying to the Lord loud and clear that we still want to be in control, that we do not trust Him to control our future lives, our past lives, or our daily lives. We may hide this hideously ugly sin under many layers of camouflage but it's still there for every one of us, as plain as the nose on our face! Everyone can see it, and everyone does! But we pretend no one can see it, not even ourselves. Wake up, oh sleeping bride of Christ! We must be ready for His coming!

The Greek word for our English word, *worry,* is *merimnao* pronounced (mer-im-nah-oh). It is the *Strong's* [1] #3309. It comes from the Greek word *merizo* which means *to divide into parts.* The word suggests *a distraction, a preoccupation with things that can and usually will cause anxiety, stress, and pressure.* All of these feelings are the distractions to entering into God's promised position of rest.

Notice that the definition states that *worry* is a preoccupation with things. We know what *occupation* is, right? It is what you do, what you make a living doing in this earth life. To occupy can mean where you live, eat, sleep, etc. So let's get this straight in our thinking. Worrying is pre-planning; pre is the prefix which means to do in advance! So a preoccupation is to go in advance to what you are doing, living, eating, sleeping, etc.

See it clearly? Whether we like to admit it or not, worrying is a choice! When we worry, we choose not to let God be God in our lives. We choose to take matters into our own pitiful human hands and try to do things ourselves. It is a hopeless and helpless choice as the Bible clearly states that worrying will never add one thing to our existence! But still many people who call themselves Christians, who profess that Jesus Christ is the Lord of their lives continue year after year to worry. So who is really Lord? Worry is lord, not Jesus Christ! When Jesus is Lord of our lives, worry is dethroned.

So the choice is yours today, as it always has been, and it always will be. As long as there is breath in our bodies, we must choose. I choose to make Jesus Christ my Lord and King. I will not worry, but will trust in my Lord and King.

Ownership:

Lord, I repent of worrying about things I can't change. I repent of worrying about things I can change but have been too self-indulgent to change. Lord, I hear Your words spoken to my heart today and I receive these words of life, helping me to break free of the stronghold of worry that I have allowed to become part of my everyday mental thought process. I say back to You the words You have said to me. I will not worry about my life, what I will eat or what I will drink; nor about my body, what I will put on. Life is more than food and the body is more than clothing. I choose to take a look at the birds of the air, for they neither sow nor gather into barns; yet my heavenly Father feeds them. I know that I am more valuable than they are to You, my Lord. I choose to say, "I will not worry," as I am understanding that this does not add one thing to my present, past, or even future life! I will not worry about clothing or natural things anymore but I will consider the lilies of the field, how they grow: they neither toil nor spin; and yet I notice that even Solomon in all his glory was not arrayed like one of these. I know Lord, that if You clothe the grass of the field, which is today, and to-morrow is thrown into the oven, You will clothe me! I have faith in You, my Lord and King! Therefore I will not worry, and say those words that feed the evil desire of my heart to take things into my own hands. I will not ask these silly, carnal questions like, "What shall I eat? What shall I drink? What shall I wear?" For You, my heavenly Father, know that I have need of all these things. I seek first the kingdom of God and Your righteousness, and all

I will not worry, but will trust in my Lord and King.

these things shall be added to me. Therefore, I will not worry about tomorrow, for tomorrow will worry about its own things. Sufficient for the day is its own trouble. I declare You are my King and Lord. There is no other. I pray in Jesus' name. Amen.

Action:

Lord, help _____ to repent of worrying about things (he/she) cannot change. By faith, I believe that _____ repents of worrying about things (he/she) can change but has been too self-indulgent to do so. Lord, I pray by faith that _____ hears Your words spoken to (his/her) heart and _____ receives these words of life, helping (him/her) to break free of the stronghold of worry that (he/she) has allowed to become a part of (his/her) everyday mental thought process. I confess to You the words You have said concerning _____. _____ will not worry about (his/her) life, what (he/she) will eat or what (he/she) will drink; nor about (his/her) body, what (he/she) will put on. Life is more than food and the body is more than clothing. Lord, I ask You to help _____ take a look at the birds of the air, for they neither sow nor gather into barns; yet You, Father feed them. _____ will know that (he/she) is more valuable than they are to You, Lord. _____ chooses to say, "I will not worry," as (he/she) understands that this does not add one thing to life! _____ will not worry about clothing or natural things anymore but (he/she) will consider the lilies of the field, how they grow: they neither toil nor spin; and yet _____ notices that even Solomon in all his glory was not arrayed like one of these. Lord, if You clothe the grass of the field, which is today, and tomorrow is thrown into the oven, You will clothe _____! _____ has faith in You,

Lord and King! Therefore, _____ will not worry, and say those words that feed the evil desire of (his/her) heart to take things into (his/her) own hands. _____ will not ask these silly, carnal questions like, "What shall I eat? What shall I drink? What shall I wear?" For You, Heavenly Father, know that _____ has need of all these things. _____ seeks first the kingdom of God and Your righteousness, and all these things shall be added to (him/her). Therefore, _____ will not worry about tomorrow, for tomorrow will worry about its own things. Sufficient for the day is its own trouble. _____ declares that You are King and Lord. There is no other. I pray in Jesus' name. Amen.

"Worry"

Greek translation:
"merimnao"

To divide into parts. The word suggests a distraction, a preoccupation with things that can and usually will cause anxiety, stress, and pressure.

Be still ...

After reading today's devotion, I examined my own permissive places of the heart. I was honest with myself about those areas that I did not really want to entrust to Him. I repented and asked Him to forgive me and strengthen me to trust Him more. Maybe you can do the same? Just be still and listen to His still, small voice. He will tell you where you have hidden things from Him, if you will let Him show you. Take the time to write Him a love note, a note of thankfulness and trust to the lover of your soul.

_____

_____

_____

_____

_____

_____

_____

_____

_____

_____

_____

_____

_____

_____

_____

_____

_____

_____

_____

_____

_____

_____

_____

Day Twenty-Two

Job 5:23-24

For you shall have a covenant with the stones of the field, and the beasts of the field shall be at peace with you. You shall know that your tent is in peace; You shall visit your dwelling and find nothing amiss.

Knowledge:

Rest. What an amazing and wonderful and glorious thought, to be at rest. So how does the above verse help us to enter into that awesome rest we long for? Is it even possible to find what our souls desire with such passionate pursuit? Rest - no strife, no turmoil, no stress, no pulling, pushing, struggling, or striving. Just think of it. In our everyday world, to actually be in covenant with the stones of the field. Okay, so that is a little bit "out there."

> *Jesus, I make You King of my home and all of my surroundings!*

But think of it this way. A covenant is a deep, committed agreement that is sometimes associated with some sort of bloodshed; giving of oneself as in the covenant of marriage, or how as a child, so many of us made a little scratch on our hands and pressed it against our friends little scratch to be blood brothers, or blood sisters! So to covenant with the stones of the field is to be in covenant with your surroundings, where you live, walk, run, breathe, eat, and sleep, and then to be in covenant with the beasts of the field, and with living, breathing things surrounding you! This would be a special place of peace ... rest with your surroundings, both breathing and non-breathing!

What follows next is a wonderful promise that you shall know that your tent, your house, your dwelling, your home is in peace. This sentence is so precious to me! Harry and I have traveled and preached the gospel for decades now. Many times, we were away from our own home for weeks at a time. In recent years, we revised our travel schedule so that we are only away from home for a week or ten days at a time. But no matter the length of the trip, I can tell you for certain, one of the most wonderful parts about traveling is getting to come back home. After a long trip, traveling and evangelizing, a great part of peace and rest is to arrive home and find nothing amiss!

I could not help but smile when I read the words, *"You shall visit your dwelling."* When you have traveled as much as we have over the years, there are many times you feel like you are "just visiting" when you come home! There were times through the years that I would wake up in the middle of the night, in my own bed at home, and not know where I was! Why? Because my bedroom at home was not laid out like a hotel room! No matter what hotel, or city, or state, or even nation you may find yourself in, the hotel rooms are all laid out alike. The bedroom is not far away from the bathroom!

I have made it my aim to wake up in my own bed and not awaken confused! I want to be at peace and rest in my dwelling. I want to be at peace and rest in my home. Jesus is the King of my home therefore; I am at rest!

Harry and I make it our goal, and we have for many years, that our home is a refuge for all who need to know and feel rest and peace for their souls. I want rest and peace; Harry wants rest and peace; we all want rest and peace! It's a promise from the Lord. Let us not fall short of entering into His rest!

Ownership:

Lord, I thank You, that You have made a way for me to be at peace and rest with all my surroundings. I accept Your Word and I shall have a covenant with the stones of the field, and the beasts of the field shall be at peace with me. I shall know that my tent is in peace and rest; I shall visit my dwelling and find nothing amiss, in the name of Jesus. Amen.

Action:

Lord, I thank You, that You have made a way for _____ to be at peace and rest with all (his/her) surroundings. _____ accepts Your Word and _____ shall have a covenant with the stones of the field, and the beasts of the field shall be at peace with _____. _____ shall know that (his/her) tent is in peace and rest; _____ shall visit (his/her) dwelling and find nothing amiss, in the name of Jesus. Amen.

Be still ...

Sometimes we just have to give up control and let God make a way for us. As we learn to accept this promise from the Lord, we may learn a few more intimate things about our own hearts. Don't be afraid to write down those things revealed by His Spirit.

_____

_____

_____

_____

_____

_____

_____

_____

_____

_____

_____

_____

_____

_____

_____

_____

_____

_____

_____

_____

_____

_____

_____

_____

_____

Day Twenty-Three

Psalm 16:7-9
I will bless the Lord who has given me counsel; My heart also instructs me in the night seasons. I have set the Lord always before me; because He is at my right hand I shall not be moved. Therefore my heart is glad and my glory rejoices; my flesh also will rest in hope.

Knowledge:

Beginning the day with, *"I will bless the Lord"* is a wonderful way to start! There are many reasons why I bless the Lord, and like David in this particular passage, He has given me counsel, and He instructs me through my own heart while I sleep. I do my very best to set the Lord always before me and I try to never forget who is my help in time of trouble. Because I do not go farther from Him than an arm's length as He is at my right hand, I will not be moved! All of these choices that are given to me to make each day, and sometimes repeatedly throughout the day, are the guidelines that help me walk in a place that causes my heart to be glad, and my glory to rejoice!

But the best part of all is when I make the right choices and when I keep the Lord first always in my life, then even my flesh can rest in hope! The context of the word *rest* in this sentence means *to dwell securely.* So I can be assured that my flesh, my physical person, my human being can dwell securely in hope. Hope is a huge part of a daily faith walk in a complete trust relationship with God. Sometimes we downplay it as it can be used incorrectly, almost like a magical word. We have all heard people say things like, "I hope everything works out." Many times, statements like these are made in context with 'wishing' rather than be-lieving. I have heard more statements of doubt and down-trodden spirits say, "I hope so." We should be saying these words as if they are the go between or the tie between what we are mentally wanting to use our faith for and be-lieve, and then truly exercising our faith in full assurance that the Lord will move the mountain of that particular sit-uation!

Faith, hope, and love are three words the Bible equates to-gether in I Corinthians 13. Like the three musketeers, these words should be interconnected in our thinking. I like to look at it as if these three are different box cars on the same train. Faith is the first box car, the engine, which is connected to the second box car of Hope, then followed by the caboose and final box car of Love. The Bible plainly says that if we must measure which is greater, by far, the last one, which is love is much greater than all the others. Why? There are so many various reasons, but let's suffice it to say without love there are not enough elements in the universe to make anything else actually work the way it was created to work!

Hope is the interconnection between where we are going and where we are right now. When we learn to live with a hopeful heart and mind, we

> *Hope connects me from where I am now, to where I am going!*

can find the rest we long for, the place to dwell with se-curity that the God of the universe, and the Lord of our lives has it all under control. We may not know the end from the beginning but He does! My knowing means nothing, but His knowing is all that is needed for me to walk out a successful, peaceful and rest-filled daily life.

Not so long ago, I was meditating on the Lord 'instructing me in the night seasons.' As I would lie down in my bed, I would pray and ask the Lord to speak to me even while I sleep. I drink a lot of water every day, which usually means I make at least one trip per night to the bathroom. On one of those trips from the bed to the 'throne,' I had taken maybe 6 or 8 steps when I realized the Lord was in mid-sentence and was talking to me! I mentally shook myself awake as I said to Him, "Lord, please forgive me. I was asleep and didn't hear what You were saying. Would You start over and tell me again?"

The Lord ever so gently told me, "I don't need you to wake up your mind. I was not talking to your mind. I was talking to your heart and spirit. Neither your heart nor your spirit need your mind to interpret for them. I have more access to your heart and spirit and they can actually hear what I am saying when your head is not in the way." Wow, what a statement! God does not always need me to be awake to talk to me. In fact, I got the distinct impression that He was saying He can get more across to my heart when I am asleep than when I am awake! I ask Him to talk to me when I sleep. Speak to my heart, Lord, without the interference of my head (mind, thoughts, and will) anytime and all the time!

My choices today are solely based upon who He is in my life, not what He does for me. He is my hope. He is my rest and my peace. He is my secure dwelling place. He is my counsel and my instructor. He is with me, and beside me. I am never alone. He is never moved and when I am holding His hand, neither am I moved. He is the One who makes my heart glad and my glory to rejoice!! Most of all, He causes my very flesh to rest in Him.

Ownership:

Lord, I will bless You, for You have given me counsel. My heart also instructs me in the night while I sleep as I am certain You speak to me, heart to heart, spirit to spirit. Even in those night seasons, when situations and circumstances make me feel like I am in the darkness, You are there, instructing and guiding me. I know that You are at my right hand and because You are never moved, I know that I can be secure in my footing while I hold Your hand. I shall not be moved. Lord, You make my heart glad. You make my glory, the very reflection of my countenance to be joyful and happy. I thank You, my Lord, that even my flesh will rest and dwell securely in hope, in Jesus' name. Amen.

Action:

Lord, _____ will bless You for You have given counsel to _____ . _____'s heart also receives instruction from You even in the night seasons. _____ has set the Lord always before (him/her). I thank You, Lord, that You are at _____'s right hand and _____ shall not be moved. Therefore, _____'s heart is glad and _____'s glory rejoices; _____'s flesh also will rest and dwell securely in hope, in Jesus' name. Amen.

Psalm 16:7-9

I will bless the Lord who has given me counsel; My heart also instructs me in the night seasons. I have set the Lord always before me; because He is at my right hand I shall not be moved. Therefore my heart is glad and my glory rejoices; my flesh also will rest in hope.

Be still ...

The Lord is calling you to sit at His side and hold His hand for a while. How long? I really don't know, but you will know as you learn to hope in Him, and be still and rest in Him. Here's a place for your prayers and thoughts.

_____

_____

_____

_____

_____

_____

_____

_____

_____

_____

_____

_____

_____

_____

_____

_____

_____

_____

_____

_____

_____

_____

_____

Day Twenty-Four

Psalm 55:6-7
So I said, "Oh, that I had wings like a dove! I would fly away and be at rest. Indeed, I would wander far off, and remain in the wilderness. Selah

Knowledge:

It is not an unusual response when we are faced with situations of trouble, trials, distress, stress, or frustrations to want to run away. I have been guilty of saying many times in actual prayer to the Lord, "Stop the world; I want to get off!" I have repeated the old Calgon® commercial many times, "Calgon, take me away!" Obviously, since we are using these very phrases in our media to sell products, we, as a society, have moments of flight instead of standing to fight through any given situation or circumstance.

Our immediate response to an actual fire is to run, as well it should be. Many times if we do not flee from the fire we get permanently burned! But God tells us through His Word that He is an all-consuming fire; so when it is the Lord Himself who is causing the heat to rise around us, we must learn to resist the urge to run away, and learn how to rest in Him no matter what is happening in our surroundings.

Even the scripture passage above ends with the word, *Selah,* which, as you remember, *means to pause and calmly think of that.* I believe the Lord would specifically want us to hear Him say, "Pause. Wait a minute and think this through, not with your head and mind, but with your heart and spirit." So, is it natural to want to escape problems, confrontations, and other things and even people who make us feel uncomfortable? Of course it is the natural response. But being the natural response does not always make it the correct response!

In John 16:33, Jesus Himself reminded us that these types of situations would be all around us in this daily, earthly environment when He said, *"These things I have spoken to you, that in Me you may have peace. In the world you will have tribulation; but be of good cheer, I have overcome the world."*

The Amplified Bible writes that passage in these words, *"...In the world you have tribulation and trials and distress and frustration..."*

None of us want to really grasp the fact that Jesus came right out and told us this world's experience would not be a cake walk. He told us that this world's experience would be filled with tribulations, trials, frustrations, and distresses! Then why do we act so put out, so offended at God when these promised scenarios actually play out in our lives? Because we don't like it, that's why! We don't like being uncomfortable. We don't like having to actually deal with daily problems that arise. We don't like to have to depend upon the Holy Spirit to help us through these things. But He has promised already that He will help us. In fact, He promised that we should actually go ahead and put on a happy face about it all, as He has already overcome any and all situations and circumstances.

Jesus plainly told all of humanity that this world would be filled with things we do not like. Even though it is the natural response to want to escape, it is not the best use of our God-given connection to simply run from things. A much more mature and wise choice would be to stand firmly in our place and wait on the Lord, and trust His Word to be true for us. Most of the time, running away is not an acceptable option. We need to learn to enter into His rest, God's kind of rest, in the midst of the turmoil surrounding us each day.

Yes, I feel like David many days and I wish for wings to fly away also. But God gave me feet to walk through situations and circumstances instead of wings to escape troubles. Someday we can escape this earth realm, but for now, we walk. And we walk hidden in Christ, hand in hand, under the shadow of the Almighty. In His presence there is fullness of joy; I can rest, no matter what is going on around me. So can you, but you must first choose to do so.

> *God gave me feet, not wings,*
> *so I will walk through trials*
> *and be victorious!*

Ownership:

Lord, thank You that You have given me an earth suit made of flesh and blood that causes my feet to stay on the ground even when my first choice is to sprout wings and fly away. I choose to be at rest in You, not as an escape from situations, but rather in knowing that You have settled all disputes concerning me. I don't have to know what is coming in my future to know that You have already settled it for me. I choose to trust You today and always. I will resist the urge to fly away, to flee from troubles and to hide in the wilderness where no one can find me. I want to be found by You, Lord. I once was lost, but now I am found, by You, in Jesus' name. Amen.

Action:

Lord, thank You that You have given _____ an earth suit made of flesh and blood that causes (his/her) feet to stay on the ground even when (his/her) first choice is to sprout wings and fly away. _____ chooses to be at rest in You, not as an escape from situations, but rather in knowing that You have settled all disputes concerning (him/her). _____ does not have to know what You are doing, or what is coming in the future to know that You, Lord, have already settled it for (him/her). Lord, I declare that _____ will trust You today and always. _____ will resist the urge to fly away, to flee from troubles and to hide in the wilderness where no one can find (him/her). _____ will be found in You, and by You, I pray. _____ once was lost, but now _____ is found, by You, in Jesus' name. Amen.

Psalm 55:6-7

So I said, "Oh, that I had wings like a
dove! I would fly away and be at rest.
Indeed, I would wander far off,
and remain in the wilderness.
Selah

Be still ...

The Lord already knows what you are going through. He knows the turmoil and trouble in your mind and heart. Talk to Him, but also, make sure you listen. He knows what you don't know, and He longs to share a secret or two with you.

Day Twenty-Five

Exodus 31:15
Work shall be done for six days, but the seventh is the Sabbath of rest, holy to the Lord. Whoever does any work on the Sabbath day, he shall surely be put to death.

Knowledge:

In our society, we have gotten far away from traditional family ways. Sources of household income have changed dramatically, even in our adult lifetimes. When I was growing up, my mama worked but she was still in our home - but 'home' was also a country store. Instead of grass out in the front yard there were gas pumps! There was a steady flow of people coming and going without knocking! We opened up the store every morning around 7 a.m., and if somebody needed something and we were not open yet, they walked around to the back door, which was the only entrance to our part of the house, and got our attention.

Yes, my mom was a stay-at-home mom, but she worked too. My dad worked as a carpenter/builder and also a farmer. Working was a huge part of my growing up experience. My sister is five years older than me, then two brothers, five and ten years younger than me. The children were expected to work, to help out, to cook, clean, farm, work the fields, hoe the garden, mow the lawn, weed the flower garden, pump the gas, check folks out in the store, and whatever else needed to be done. We were not *told* to do it. We were *expected* to do it, therefore we did it!

In our generation, I find my own method of parenting is not nearly as effective as my parents'. There are many reasons, and not nearly enough pages in this book to cover the 'why that is' discussion. Let's suffice it to say the rules were plain, and the punishment and correction for disobedience was also plain. As a parent, I find the hardest part is not making the rules, but enforcing the rules. I used to think that would be the easier part but how wrong I was!

It's quite easy for Harry and me to tell our children what to do, what not to do, what we expect, etc. Then the hard part kicks in ... when they don't do what we expect! The discipline is not just in disciplining (which means making disciples!) our children, but in disciplining ourselves to stick to the plan. It is much easier on the parents to simply give in and let up on the correction. But does that do any of us any good at all? Hardly! And as the old saying goes, "We get what we pay for."

I am not saying that as a society we have not been hard enough on our children. But I am saying that as a society of parents maybe we have not been quite hard enough on ourselves. We are quite self-indulgent as a whole, and we don't like to follow through on anything!

So how does any of this relate to the scripture? It's all about prioritizing. This one verse is taken out of an entire portion of scripture dealing with the dedication and discipline of the children of Israel to stay strong in the midst of adversity and to build the tabernacle for the Lord. Was it more discipline then to continue to work on the Sabbath that had already been set aside as holy unto the Lord? Or did it take more discipline, more self-discipline, mental and spiritual discipline, more discipline of their faith walk to trust the Lord as they honored Him by obeying Him to rest, and set aside this holy day as unto Him? They were showing their own discipline to obey when not rationally understanding the outcome.

In what way am I speaking? The Bible is clear that we are to set aside a day for Him out of every seven days to totally and completely think about, meditate on, and rest, yes, rest in Him. And yet even on our 'Sabbath' day do we really rest? Do we really discipline ourselves to give this day 100% to Him? Does God have our attention all day long one day a week? Does He have our undivided loyalty, devotion, trust, commitment, and even physical stillness one day out of every seven?

I won't even go into the actual physical benefits of learning how to be still, and rest our flesh, our minds, emotions one day out of every seven, but there is so much research and proof of the good outcome in this that we should obey this command, if not for anything else, for our own peace of mind and health of our flesh. Oh, don't get me wrong here. I know I am preaching to the choir, and that choir is myself!

As I write these words by the Spirit of God flowing through me, I am writing convicting words to my own mind and flesh. My own spirit wants to stop typing and take a little time to fall on my knees and ask the Lord to forgive me of my own self-willed disobedience to the things of God that are meant for my benefit. In fact, I think I will take a moment to do just that; won't you join me on your knees at His feet?

> *Stop,*
> *Take a moment to*
> *worship Jesus at*
> *His feet.*

Okay, I'm back. There is not much to tell. I have no excuses as to why I disobey the Lord in this area. You probably don't have any 'real' excuses either. So let's just get over ourselves and repent. We'll cover this in our prayer in a few more pages.

I don't want to stop this devotional without addressing the punishment for the crime of not resting, mentioned in the scripture. Of course, in our society we do not put people to death for not resting on the Sabbath. If that were still a punishable offense, I daresay there would be no one left to actually carry out the punishment! So we have all sinned and fallen short of the glory of God. Yes, we have, and thank God we have a way back to His throne, back to His feet, to worship Him because of Jesus Christ, the Messiah, God's own Son, who was sent to make a way for us. We could not pay the price of this horrible sin so He paid it for us.

But in a practical way, maybe the Lord is telling us that when we do not obey His command to rest, we are 'killing' ourselves. Maybe we have destroyed our own minds, emotions and even our flesh bodies by not obeying Him. Does He punish us with this? I don't believe so, but I believe when we choose to disobey Him, the law that is set forth in motion from the time it is spoken out of the mouth of God is self-fulfilling.

What am I saying? I am saying that there are reasons why we can't sleep, can't rest, and continually fight health issues within the body of Christ. There are huge reasons why, when a time of prayer goes forth in any church, within the boundaries of any denomination, sickness and disease is a huge attack within God's own body and bride. Could this be a simple result of us breaking God's law of rest? I believe we are breaking that law, and I believe we are paying the price for it in our flesh bodies, our mental capacities, our marriages, and families and even in our churches and society. We are a sick and dying society because we do not know how to rest.

Rest is a law and it still holds true today. Gravity is a law and it is still in effect. When it's broken badly enough, it is punishable by death. What do I mean by this? No matter how much you love the Lord, no matter how sold out to Him you are, no matter how much you pray and worship Him, if you step off a high story building you will most probably die or at the least be seriously injured, all by your own breaking of the law of gravity. We know this; we understand it, and any person in their right mind does not have to test this law to know it works. So maybe we should take the same attitude toward God's law of rest.

Work for six days but on the seventh day, rest, for it is holy unto the Lord.

Ownership:

Lord, I have no excuses that can withstand Your law of rest. There is nothing in me that can put forth an argument of any validity against why I have chosen over and over again to break this law. All I can say is thank You for sending Your Son, Jesus Christ, whom I serve and to whom I belong, to stand in the gap as my intercessor and redeemer. I ask You, Father, to forgive me when I break Your law of rest. I ask You, Lord, to forgive me for trying to work my way into salvation. Forgive me for trying to work my way into 'feeling good about myself.' And Lord, forgive me when I am more driven to work, than I am drawn to worship You. I repent and I ask You to remit my punishment and heal my flesh, bring peace and rest to my mind, will, and emotions. I love You, Lord, and I set aside time each day to worship You; I set the seventh day aside to rest in You and worship You. Thank You for forgiving me and helping me to not be driven back to work on the seventh day. Thank You for strengthening me and showing me Your salvation from my foolishness, in Jesus' name. Amen.

Entering Rest - Be Still

Action:

Lord, I ask You to forgive _____ for disobeying Your law of rest. I ask You to reveal to (him/her) that You can make a way through Jesus Christ to obey You in this for (his/her) benefit. Lord, I thank You for Jesus Christ, who stands in the gap for _____ concerning this. Lord, I pray that You strengthen and help _____ to understand and obey You in all things including learning through Your Spirit how to rest. Teach _____ by Your Spirit that obedience is better than sacrificing (his/her) own flesh. Lord, please forgive _____ when (he/she) is more driven to work, than allowing You to draw (him/her) to Your presence. Thank You for forgiving _____ and helping _____ to rest in You and worship You. Thank You for strengthening _____ and showing (him/her) Your salvation from the foolish thoughts of disobedience, in Jesus' name. Amen.

Be still ...

Too many times, we approach the Lord with an agenda instead of simply to enjoy His presence. Why don't you lay aside any specifics you might feel you want or need while you pray? Be still and listen to Him. If what you gain is the feeling of His embrace or the warmth of His breath upon your cheek, could you ask for anything more?

Day Twenty-Six

Exodus 33:12-14
Then Moses said to the Lord, "See, You say to me, 'Bring up this people.' But You have not let me know whom You will send with me. Yet You have said, 'I know you by name, and you have also found grace in My sight.'
"Now therefore, I pray, if I have found grace in Your sight, show me now Your way, that I may know You and that I may find grace in Your sight. And consider that this nation is Your people." And He said, "My Presence will go with you, and I will give you rest."

Knowledge:

The Lord declares to us, *"My Presence will go with you, and I will give you rest."* Honestly, what more could we ask? There are two things that can bring about what we long for offered in this promise from the Lord. First, the Lord promises that His presence will go with us wherever we go, and second, He will give us rest! So just from this statement alone, we see that rest is from God, and it is a gift!

I can't earn rest, nor can I buy it. I can't have it without it being given to me, and the rest I long for must come as a gift from my Father God! Simple, and yet, quite over-whelming, in that God's kind of rest can't be controlled, or manipulated by me, or any other human being. There is no pill that I can take, or three-step formula that I can com-plete that will produce the rest I must have to live in peace, safety, security, and wholeness.

We must sound like Moses to the Father God at times

when we come to Him in prayer saying, "See, Lord, I bring You myself. Here I am, but I am still waiting on a plan and details from You. Just when do You suppose You are going to let me in on the details of my future?" We rehearse to the Lord His promises just as Moses did when he said to God, *"You have said that You know me by name, and I have found grace in Your sight."* Sometimes we go on and on in prayer trying to convince God Almighty of things, as if we know something He does not know!

We follow our obvious attempts to manipulate, convince, control our situations and circumstances, with the sound of humble words like "Lord, if I have found favor in Your sight, show me Your plan, Your way, that I may find grace in Your sight." We go on and on, but our own heart is condemning us most of the time for we are not content to simply walk out the plans of the Lord as He gives them to us. We are manipulated by trying to please others, by trying to show how much we know God when we get the plans before others get the plans! (Sigh...) Can you hear me sigh at my own weaknesses? Our own hearts bring about the results of God's mercy and truth, and even grace toward us, for our humanness is always more about us, and our glory than it is about others, and the Lord's glory. I repent of trying to know more than I need to know. I am learning that with the Lord I am on a need-to-know basis, and most of the time, I don't need to know to obey Him!

> *I am on a need-to-know basis with You, Lord, but I don't need to know, in order to obey You!*

In spite of our pitiful attempts to try and get the Lord to come around to our way of thinking, as we plead for the Lord to consider this nation as His nation, the Lord loves us so very much. When we talk the talk of a godly nation, but our actions, decisions and society tell a much different story and paint a much more explicit picture of who we really are, Lord forgive us, heal us, and restore us. Even in these dire times in which we are living, the Lord continues to uphold the righteous and give grace to this nation, our states, communities, families, marriages, and homes. So with an undeserved condition of heart and life, we boldly declare what He has promised us, "Lord, Your presence will go with us, and give us rest."

Ownership:

Lord, I come before You just as Moses did and I pray, "Lord, see, You say to me, 'Bring up this people.' I bring myself before You. I present my life as the only viable gift I have to give You. Forgive me when my prayers are filled with the conjunction 'but' as if You owe me anything. Forgive me when I try and manipulate and control my situations and circumstances instead of trusting You with the outcome. Forgive me when I want to know Your plans and details for my life before I am truly ready in my heart. Thank You, Lord, for You know me by name, and I have found grace in Your sight. I thank You, Lord, that I know You and You know me by name. Lord, I ask that You give this nation grace and mercy and that You consider this nation as Your people. Lord, I receive Your promise that Your presence will go with me, and You will give me rest, in Jesus' name. Amen."

Action:

Lord, I come before You and I confess that _____ is willing to give (himself/herself) to You, and to present (his/her) life to You. Forgive _____ when (his/her) prayers are filled with more 'but' words than 'trust' words. Forgive _____ when knowingly and unknowingly (he/she) tries to manipulate Your will and plans for (his/her) life. Lord, help _____ to be patient with the details and plans that You have for (his/her) future. Thank You, Lord, that You know _____ by name, and that You have given grace to _____. Lord, _____ receives Your promise that Your presence will go with (him/her) and You will give (him/her) rest, in Jesus' name. Amen.

Exodus 33:14

"My Presence will go with you,
and I will give you rest."

Be still ...

We are all on a need-to-know basis with the Lord, and when we need to know any details of our lives, He will tell us. Can you simply trust Him today in knowing this? You might be like me in that you need a little space to write down those times you threw a spiritual fit and demanded details of your future, when all you really needed to do was trust Him. Here are a few lines for you to vent a prayer of forgiveness, instead of frustration. Listen, be still, and obey. He will tell you what you need to know today.

_____

_____

_____

_____

_____

_____

_____

_____

_____

_____

_____

_____

_____

_____

_____

_____

_____

_____

_____

_____

Day Twenty-Seven

Isaiah 66:1-2

"Heaven is My throne, and earth is My footstool. Where is the house that you will build Me? And where is the place of My rest? For all those things My hand has made, and all those things exist," says the Lord. "But on this one will I look; on him who is poor and of a contrite spirit, and who trembles at My word."

Knowledge:

In Acts 7:49-50, Stephen quoted this passage from Isaiah as a living proof testimony that God's ultimate plan was to never dwell in buildings or manmade temples, but rather in the hearts and daily lives of people. How often do we hear the Lord say to us throughout each day, "Let Me live in you." I hear Him calling to me to yield to Him so many times. Sometimes I give in and give up control and other times, as I look back over my life, I have had to 'do it my way.' Of course, these times have always cost me more than I could afford to pay in various forms. I have lost my peace, my rest, my comfort and security in His presence more times than I care to admit, all because of my stubborn and rebellious heart.

> *Yes Lord, come live in me!*

The Hebrew word for *rest* in this scripture is the same word we have discussed earlier. It is the word *menuchah*. It means *a resting place, a place of stillness, repose, consolation, peace and rest.* It is a quiet place. The Lord is simply asking in this scripture for us to allow Him to move into our very 'human being' and set up His presence within us. He is calling us to become His resting place, and in response to our allowing Him to take over our 'being' we get in return His kind of rest, peace, security, stillness, repose, consolation, and wholeness. When He lives in me, then my self-willed, self-focused, selfish person must move out! Rebellion cannot live in the same house with submission and obedience. Rest and peace cannot live in the same house as chaos and confusion.

When we can actually see ourselves as the resting place of God, the house of the Lord, we can begin to understand the eternal benefits of becoming one with His presence. All those things that try and steal our health, peace, and wholeness, like sickness, disease, strife, chaos, confusion, etc. must move out! Light and dark cannot exist together! I want to be God's resting place. I want Him to find within my being, His place to dwell.

No matter what is going on around us daily, we can still choose to allow the Lord to come into our house and set up His kind of housekeeping. I don't know about you, but I am quite certain that I need the Lord's presence to keep my house in order. I can't do it myself. I have failed too many times to count, so I willingly turn my being over to the King of Kings. I invite His presence to move into every place within me, and take over! How about you? Are you tired of trying and failing on your own? He is waiting to move into your being and set you up as His house that you have built for Him.

Ownership:

Lord, Your Word is plain when You say that heaven is Your throne and earth is Your footstool. And when You ask me, "Where is the house that you have built Me?" I can answer You and say, "Right here, Lord. Here is my life, my mind, will, and emotions. Here is my spirit, soul, and body. All of me is Yours. Please live in me and find the resting place for Your presence. I know You make everything and by You, everything exists. I want You to look down from Your holy place and find me, the one who is humble and broken before You. Lord, I tremble at Your Word. My life is Yours. Let me be Your resting place, in Jesus' name. Amen."

Action:

Lord, Your Word is specific when You say that heaven is Your throne and earth is Your footstool. When You ask, "Where is the house that _____ has built Me?" may (his/her) answer be, "Right here in my heart." Lord, I ask for You to move into _____'s life and heart right now. Show _____ how much You long to live within (him/her). Lord, I ask that You find Your resting place inside _____'s heart and daily life. _____ knows You make everything and by You, everything exists. I ask that You look down from Your holy habitation and find _____, humble and broken before You. _____ trembles at Your Word, Lord. I confess that _____'s life is Yours. Rest in _____, in Jesus' name. Amen.

Be still ...

Allow the Lord to set up housekeeping within your soul. Allow the Holy Spirit to take over the controls of your life. Be still and listen. He is the Word. He is always saying something. Don't be in such a big hurry. Write down what He tells you.

_____

_____

_____

_____

_____

_____

_____

_____

_____

_____

_____

_____

_____

_____

_____

_____

_____

_____

_____

_____

_____

_____

_____

_____

_____

_____

Day Twenty-Eight

Isaiah 14:7
The whole earth is at rest and quiet; they break forth into singing.

Knowledge:

What a wonderful scripture to pray every day over ourselves personally, our families and friends, our nation, and

> *I declare that I am at rest and quiet!*

the whole world! What a tremendous thought that the whole earth is at rest and quiet, that the whole earth breaks forth into singing! What a joyous day this will be! Don't mistakenly think that this is a pipe dream! It is not a pipe dream, but a reality in the future for God's people. Think about it this way. Everything in the future is simply a past event, a historical event, that has not happened yet! So with that deep thought in mind, consider this scripture as prophecy that can be fulfilled ahead of time in our hearts and minds!

> *And when I am not quite there yet, Lord, help me get there!*

I have heard many Christian people make statements like, "I've read the last chapter and we win." Well, in Christ, this is absolutely true. So the real question is, "Are you in Christ or do you just talk about being in Christ?" Because if you are in Christ you can go ahead and rejoice, and let go of worry, fretting, and stress, because the whole earth is at rest and quiet! The whole earth breaks forth into singing!

You might be thinking, "Well, obviously you are not living at my house, or in my situation!" That's true, I don't know what you are going through. I don't know the details of the pain you are suffering. But I do know the outcome of it all. I believe the Bible is true. I believe every word of it is prophetic and inside of Christ Jesus, it is finished! Which means that no matter what I am looking at on a daily basis, or what I am feeling, or what kind of thoughts are trying to bombard my mind to steal, kill, and destroy me, it cannot win. Nothing can defeat me as long as I am hidden in Christ!

Is this a little too 'cheerleading/rah, rah' for you? Well, apparently, it is not too much for the Lord! This passage of scripture in Isaiah is about Israel, God's own people, returning from the captivity of Babylon. Throughout history we can see this event unfold before our eyes, but we also can see similar events happening around us every day. We can also know that these types of events will always be happening or about to happen as long as the earth remains. Until Jesus comes and sets up His kingdom reign on the earth, the spirit of Babylon (Lucifer himself) will be trying to take from God's people. The spirit of the antichrist will continually try to take back that little piece of land we call the nation of Israel.

There will be wars and rumors of wars from now until the end of time as we know it. But the good news is the Lord has already won this battle. Even before it is fought, He has won! Israel, God's chosen people, and those of us who are adopted into the family, will always come out of Babylon. Israel will always be restored, and this taunting song will be sung against Babylon, the spirit of the antichrist, that ol' fallen devil, Lucifer. The king of Babylon symbolizes a specific ruler, or rulers, but mostly all evil rulers, demonic forces, and antichrist spirits. God's people will always rule and reign in victory because we belong to the victor, Jesus Christ! Whether it is a past event, a present event unfolding before our eyes, or a future event not yet reached on this earth's timeline, we will sing the taunting song of victory as we declare the whole earth is at rest and quiet. We will break forth and sing the song of the victorious! Why don't you sing along with us right now? Come on, sing it loudly! Only all of heaven is waiting and listening to the victorious sounds coming forth from your being! Sing and break forth into victorious, restful living! Go ahead! Sing like no one's listening!

Ownership:

Lord, I give You my whole earth experience. I give You my life, past, present and future. I make a commitment to declare to my world and my daily earthly life that I am at rest and quiet. I cannot come out of it, as I am hidden inside of rest and quiet, and rest and quiet is hidden inside of me. Because I already have driven out the spirit of stress through the victory I have obtained in Jesus, I now enter into God's kind of rest. I break forth into singing the song of victorious rest, in Jesus' name. Amen.

Action:

Lord, I give You _____ and I present (his/her) life before You. I declare and stand in the gap for (him/her) to give You (his/her) life, past, present, and future. I ask You Lord, to continue to knock on the door of _____'s heart so that entrance can be gained to bring about rest and quiet in (his/her) daily earthly life. I declare that _____ is at rest and quiet in You, and that _____ breaks forth into singing, in Jesus' name. Amen.

Be still ...

There is a song of victory inside your heart. It's there, but you have to let it out. Don't be afraid. The Lord is with you; He will never leave you nor forsake you. Most of all, He wants to teach you to break forth into singing so His rest and His quiet can take over your life. It's up to you. Can you trust Him that much?

_____

_____

_____

_____

_____

_____

_____

_____

_____

_____

_____

_____

_____

_____

_____

_____

_____

_____

_____

_____

_____

_____

_____

_____

_____

_____

Day Twenty-Nine

Jeremiah 6:16
Thus says the Lord: "Stand in the ways and see, and ask for the old paths, where the good way is, and walk in it; then you will find rest for your souls. But they said, 'We will not walk in it.'

Knowledge:

Here is another wonderful scripture where the Lord is talking to us. God is specifically talking to us and telling us what to do in this verse! God says to stand in the ways and see. Ask for the old paths. Just for a minute, let's stop and take a look because the Lord says to stand in the way and see! Take a look! Don't stand around blindly missing what the Lord is saying to us! Look! See! Then He plainly says to ask for the old paths. What could this mean? Have you ever heard the phrase, "If it ain't broke, don't fix it." How about, "Why reinvent the wheel?" I believe the Lord is saying there are things in His Word that point to paths of righteousness, and here He is telling us to look for those old well-worn paths of righteousness and walk that same road that can produce the good ways with good results.

Once we see the right path, and find the right path, then it is our responsibility to walk that path. When we do, then we can find rest for our souls. This is a great promise for peace and rest for our minds, wills, emotions, and our hearts! Rest is offered from our tumultuous emotions! Wow, for a woman to get a rest, a break from her emotions… that is total and complete rest! For a man to get a break from his mind, that's rest! Sometimes our emotions can drive us on a road we don't even want to be on, but when we allow ourselves to get on that emotional path it's hard to get off of it! So the bottom line then is to not get on that emotional roller coaster in the first place! The Lord is telling us to look for the well-worn path, and then walk that way! Once we find a path that is established and leads to a restful destination, then when we take that same path we can expect to get to the same restful destination.

Rest and peace are God's kind of righteousness. His paths are well-worn and always bring about a humble and broken spirit before Him without the driving force of pride! His ways are not the natural ways we might normally choose but when we seek His way, we find His destination, and can fulfill His promises.

I want this path to be so well-worn in my life that all who come after me can easily find the ruts that I have made. My heart's desire is to have worn a path so plainly marked out that my children and grandchildren can follow right behind me. Where am I going? I am going to rest in His arms as He beckons me to come to Him. I will go and He will give me rest. I long for Him. He longs for me. He longs for you too. Will you come when He calls? Listen! He is calling you right now!

Let go of any and all paths that are not leading you to His destination of rest. Let go of any past trails that have never taken you where you really want to go. Follow His steps. He is leading… will you follow Him?

Ownership:

Lord, I will obey You and stand where You tell me to stand and see what You want me to see; I will ask for the old paths, where the good way is, and I will walk in it. I will find rest for my soul. I will not be like those who make the wrong choice. I will not follow those who will not walk in the path of righteousness. I will walk in those deep ruts of righteousness made by the righteous who have gone before me, in Jesus' name. Amen.

Action:

Lord, I thank You that _____ will obey You and stand where You tell (him/her) to stand. _____ will see what You tell (him/her) to see. _____ will ask for the old paths, where the good way is, and (he/she) will walk in it. _____ will find rest for (his/her) soul. _____ will not be like those who make the wrong choice. _____ will not follow those who will not walk in the path of righteousness. _____ will walk in those deep ruts made by the righteous ones who have gone before (him/her), in Jesus' name. Amen.

Be still ...

It's not too hard to follow in the path that others have made. So as you approach the Lord's throne today, simply ask Him to show you the way. I believe He will show you what you need to see, and teach you what you need to know. Don't be afraid to write it down. Some thoughts revealed by the Spirit cannot be easily grasped until meditated on for a while. Take your time.

_____

_____

_____

_____

_____

_____

_____

_____

_____

_____

_____

_____

_____

_____

_____

_____

_____

_____

_____

_____

_____

_____

_____

_____

Day Thirty

II Corinthians 12:9-10
And He said to me, "My grace is sufficient for you, for My strength is made perfect in weakness." Therefore most gladly I will rather boast in my infirmities, that the power of Christ may rest upon me. Therefore I take pleasure in infirmities, in reproaches, in needs, in persecutions, in distresses, for Christ's sake. For when I am weak, then I am strong.

Knowledge:

For the statement above, *"For when I am weak, then I am strong,"* to be in effect, I must first welcome the power of Christ to rest upon me. How I long for the power of Christ that raised the dead, and healed the sick, and forgave sins, to rest upon me daily! One of my most favorite parts of the above scripture is that I do not have to earn God's grace or even His power.

I have spent a lot of time asking the Lord to remove many things, people, events, pain, etc. from my life. I have probably wasted much effort trying to get the Lord to do something when I could have been allowing His power to simply rest upon me in the midst of my circumstances and situations. I, like Paul in this passage of scripture, am learning to take pleasure in infirmities, reproaches, needs, persecutions, and distresses. I can't say that I am there yet, but I am learning to be there. I want to rest in the Lord and allow Him to rest upon me, no matter what I am going through at the time.

Over the past few years, I have had more opportunities to

trust in the resting place of the Lord upon my life, most recently with my last surgery to remove another section of my colon. The first time I had to have my colon resectioned because of cancer, I had so many warnings, symptoms, sickness, etc. I was weak, tired, and physically worn out, after a year-long battle for our youngest child, our only daughter who was battling an inoperable brain tumor. While she was going through eleven months of the worst battle, I began to have symptoms that were highly problematic, and pointed directly to a serious problem. But I did not have time to fight two wars at once. We stood strong for Gabrielle, until November 23, 1999, when she took her last breath on this side and began to breathe of heaven's air, filled with the glory of God.

Within a few days, my physical symptoms worsened and I was back on the front lines of a battle for my own life. Three months to the day after Gabrielle crossed over to heaven, I was on an operating table, having colon resection surgery and removal of the cancerous tumor.

Seven years later, in a routine colonoscopy, another suspicious area was discovered, this time without any symptoms or warnings of any kind. I found myself battling, again, for restoration in my physical body. This scripture became a prayer, a cry of my heart toward the throne of God. Maybe that is why I have so boldly proclaimed the healing power of God in my life for so many years, that as I boast in my infirmities, the power of Christ may rest upon me!

I am quite certain that I cannot live as successfully for Jesus without His power resting, "tenting" over me! It is by His grace, His power, His presence that I live and breathe and have my being! I do not try to hide my problems, or pretend like I have no trials. How silly we are to think that the kingdom of God can only be seen in the lives of those with no troubles! For it is in my weakness that others can see His strength and power in my life. I do not hide behind the lie that I could never have a problem. This is a very delusional and immature way of trying to live the Christian life. The real power rests in knowing that even if all hell is sent to bring us down, that Christ's power rests upon us in the deepest and darkest times of trouble.

So here I am once again, saying the same thing. Whether you see us in person ministering the power of Christ, read one of our books, or listen to one of my music CDs, hear the power of Christ resting upon me, as we proclaim for all the world to see and hear, *"God's grace is sufficient for me!"* For even when I am at my weakest and most vulnerable point, God's power through Christ dwells within me, tents over me, covering me with His grace. I do not long to do anything myself. I want no glory for anything, except to glory in the power of Christ and Him alone. Jehovah Nissi, His banner, covering, tent over me is love and here in His shadow, I find rest.

> God's grace
> is sufficient.
> Period.

Ownership:

Lord, I say to You what You said to Paul in Your Word. Your grace is sufficient for me, for Your strength is made perfect in my weakness. Therefore, as Paul so appropriately declared these words, I most gladly will boast in my infirmities, that the power of Christ may rest upon me. Therefore, I take pleasure in infirmities, in reproaches, in needs, in persecutions, in distresses, for Christ's sake. For when I am weak, then I am strong. I know by the power of Christ within me that nothing is by my own strength but by the strength of my Lord and Savior, in Jesus' name. Amen.

Action:

Lord, I ask that Your power rest upon _____. I thank You, that Your grace is sufficient for _____, for Your strength is made perfect in _____'s weakness. _____ will most gladly boast in (his/her) infirmities, that Your power may rest upon (him/her). Give _____ the strength (he/she) needs to take pleasure in infirmities, reproaches, needs, persecutions, and distresses for Your sake. When _____ is weak, then (he/she) is strong, by the power of Christ, who rests upon (him/her), in Jesus' name. Amen.

God's grace is sufficient for me!

"Grace"

Greek translation:
"charis"
Unmerited favor, undeserved
blessing, a free gift.

"Sufficient"

Greek translation:
"arkeo"
Raising a barrier. Warding off.

Be still ...and rest in the Lord.

Ask the Lord in your own words for the power of Christ to rest upon you, to cover you, to raise a barrier and put a tent over you so you can settle down and listen to His still, small voice. Ask Him to speak to you. He will. He is the Word made flesh and dwelling among us. Just listen.

_____

_____

_____

_____

_____

_____

_____

_____

_____

_____

_____

_____

_____

_____

_____

_____

_____

_____

_____

_____

_____

_____

_____

_____

_____

_____

_____

_____

Day Thirty-One

Hebrews 4:9-10
There remains therefore a rest for the people of God. For he who has entered His rest has himself also ceased from his works as God did from His.

Knowledge:

As I was typing the above verse, I heard the Lord say for me to go back through one of my older files of sermon notes. At the time, I had it in my mind what the Lord wanted me to find, but when I opened this huge notebook filled with my handwritten notes I saw more of what He wanted me to share with you. Why is rest so important for us? If we don't rest in God, we get so stressed out by the cares of life that we fall into unbelief and disobedience. In the margins of my notes there are some very interesting statements and comments. One such statement is, "How not to be a failure!" The devil tried to get us to think that we failed God because of things we have gone through, for example, the car wreck in 1968, the miscarriage of our baby in the early '90's, the 7 months I spent flat on my back in bed waiting for the arrival of our fourth child, Gabrielle. These were not failures, they were actually great successes in my life. We tend to celebrate the triumphant moments of visual victories, but we do not celebrate the journeys that lead us to the victories.

I will speak the outcome of victory!

I succeeded because I survived and made it to the other side of each trial and troubled time. I am not a failure; I am a success. I am learning to speak the outcome of victory no matter what stage of the journey that I am in.

Hebrews 4:11 states, *"Let us therefore be zealous and exert ourselves and strive diligently to enter that rest of God, to know and experience it for ourselves, that no one may fall or perish by the same kind of unbelief and disobedience into which those in the wilderness fell."* (AMP)

Apparently, there is a rest offered to us by God, and that promise remains even now. But when we read verse 11, we see how to enter God's promise of rest, and this 'how-to' given is most probably why so many people do not enter it. We must *'... be zealous and exert ourselves.'* Well, we can stop right there, for most people will not do anything that requires zeal and exertion! This is an effect of the effort of discipline and let's face it, we live in an undisciplined, take-the-easy-way, world. If it's not quick and easy, then most likely, it will not get done in our society.

There is nothing in God's realm that would sell in our drive-through/microwave society, for God clearly states through His Word, *"to him who endures to the end..."* (Matthew 24:13). It is endurance, standing fast, not giving up or giving in, having a disciplined mentality that finishes the course and runs the race of life, that God rewards.

So what is the answer? Do we simply give in and go the way of the rest of the world? Hardly! Failure is not an option! Even with the promise of rest we must enter this journey to rest with the desired result already manifested in our faith, our thought life, and our vision. We must not stop this journey of God's kind of rest until we are living in this promise, and this promise is living in us.

Just a few more lines of my notes on the subject of rest.

We human beings need to be delivered from the 'death row' of worry and fear. People are dying prematurely because of worry and fear. The physical body carries sickness upon it because of worry and fear. Work belongs to God. Burdens belong to Jesus. Work and burdens are carried by those who will not enter into God's promise of rest. When we don't enter the promise then we are embracing the curse, which is the opposite of the promise. Galatians 3:13 clearly states that we are redeemed from the curse, including the curse of worry, fear, and flesh works that do not produce the eternal effects of kingdom living.

God does not need our help. He does not need it or want it, and we can't really help Him anyway. We get in the way of His plan, like Abraham and Sarah did when they tried to help the Lord. Ishmael became a permanent part of their lives, and family, and even in our world today we are still living with the negative effects of humans who tried to help the plan of God! Do we really want to be responsible for messing up the human race with our over-inflated egos, to think that we need to help God?

I am reminded of a time I had with the Lord many years ago. I was sitting in a conference listening to a speaker when all of a sudden I heard the voice of the Lord say to me, "When did I create mankind?"

Being the type of person who loves to show off how much knowledge I have, I immediately said, "On the sixth day." The Lord quickly responded to me, "What time of the day?"

Well, I was taken aback. I was not sure what time of day mankind was created. My mind raced, my thoughts were searching the crevices of gray matter in my brain for any recollection of a time being given in the creation of the human race. I answered, "Lord, I don't know what time." The Lord simply responded to me, "Look it up." Of course, I knew the Lord meant for me to open my Bible and read the passage of scripture where it was clearly stated, *"So the evening..."* There it was. Mankind was God's last creation at the end of the sixth day. The Lord stated ever so softly to me, "If I had needed you to do anything, I would have created you earlier in the week."

Wow, what a profound kick in the stomach of a 'doer' personality, like myself, who is always trying to win the approval of everyone, including the Lord, by how much I do! So the Lord's seventh day which was set aside solely for the purpose of rest, which He did not need but He wanted, was our (human beings) first full day of existence. And what was the purpose of that first full day designated for humanity? The first thing the Lord designed and purposed for us was to rest ... rest ... rest ... with Him.

We were not created to work; we were created to rest with Him, and in Him. We were created to be with Him. Please do not misunderstand me. I am not saying we do not need jobs. Of course we do. There are too many scriptures that support working and eating! These are not the essential parts of 'work' of which I am speaking. And I believe you know this revelation even as I write it to you. This is about our attitudes toward God, our Creator. This is about how we approach life and our parts of the puzzle of life. God longs for us to learn how to rest in the midst of the worst kinds of problems, trials, frustrations, situations, and circumstances. Why? Because rest is ordained and still holds today. Rest is a promised part of God's plan for our success here on this earth. Learning how to rest in God is one of the greatest keys to real and long lasting success in life.

I will leave you today with a few more nuggets from my notes on rest.

So....

Quit worrying and being afraid, start trusting God.

Quit telling God how to do everything, start trusting God.

Quit trying to help God, start trusting God.

Quit doubting His ability to get the job done, start trusting God.

Quit rehearsing the problems to God and everyone else, start trusting God.

Ownership:

Lord, I hear You when You say in Your Word there remains a rest for me, for I am Yours. I belong to You. I am Your people. And for me who has entered Your rest, I have ceased from my own works as You, God, did from Yours. I willfully obey Your voice and I enter Your rest for me right now, in Jesus' name. Amen.

Action:

Lord, Your Word states that there remains a rest for _____, who is Your people. For _____ who has entered Your rest has ceased from (his/her) own works of the flesh. Lord, You rest, therefore _____ rests. _____ will obey Your voice and enter Your rest, in Jesus' name. Amen.

Be still ...

Relax. It's not up to you. This is God's, and I truly believe that, "He's got it!" If we can't trust God, then we can't trust anybody or anything! So let go, and go ahead... enter into God's kind of rest. Don't forget to write down parts of the journey. You may be like me, and years later find yourself right back in the same place on the circle of life, needing to go back and read what you wrote today.

_____

_____

_____

_____

_____

_____

_____

_____

_____

_____

_____

_____

_____

_____

_____

_____

_____

_____

_____

_____

_____

I QUIT!

I determine in my heart to . . .

Quit worrying and being afraid -
start trusting God.
Quit telling God how to do everything -
start trusting God.
Quit trying to help God -
start trusting God.
Quit doubting His ability to
get the job done -
start trusting God.
Quit rehearsing the problems to
God and everyone else -
start trusting God.

Day Thirty-Two

I Chronicles 28:2,6
Then King David rose to his feet and said, "Hear me, my brethren and my people: I had it in my heart to build a house of rest for the ark of the covenant of the Lord, and for the footstool of our God, and had made preparations to build it.

"Now He said to me, 'It is your son Solomon who shall build My house and My courts; for I have chosen him to be My son, and I will be his Father...'

Knowledge:

Isn't it wonderful to realize that the Lord is not relying solely on you to get the kingdom business done? I love the realization that He does not need me; He wants me! I love the revelation that I am not the only one working for the kingdom of God and the harvest of the Lord is not dependent upon me only! We, like David, are at the season of life, when our sons are becoming of age. Our sons are becoming young men and their futures are being ordered of the Lord.

It has always been my mindset that I must do everything, literally everything, necessary to insure the coming of the Lord! It is not wrong to live a holy life, to be found acceptable to the Lord, but when our thoughts and our mindset only sees a mirror reflection of ourselves, and does not realize the body and bride of Christ is made up of multitudes, we have missed God's perspective of kingdom thinking and being. I long to see myself as a cell inside the body and bride of Christ, not me, myself, and I as the only reflection I see.

I had it in my heart just as David did, to build a house of rest for the Lord and I will do that for Him, but this house that I build for His presence is my person, my body, soul, and spirit. This person is His house of rest and I make it my one ambition to continue to stay in this place of rest with Him and for Him! I want to be like David in that God used him generationally. David reared a son named Solomon, whom God chose to build His physical house and courts where the ark of the covenant could reside; this place of rest for the ark would mean it did not have to be in a tent traveling around the country any longer.

Our job is to not only house the Spirit of God, and give Him a place of rest within our own person, but we are also to raise up a generation to follow us where the Spirit of God can also rest. Of course, that generation includes our sons, Harry III and Roman, but it is not only those two men of God. We are to raise up a generation coming after us of people who are willing to lay it all down to be a temple, a tabernacle, a body, and a bride for His glory, His power, and His presence to reside within, and rest upon!

I have spent years worrying and fretting over the things that I have been 'doing' for God, but I can recall the many times I have heard the voice of the Lord say to me, "You are not the only one working for My kingdom." Over the years of serving the Lord, I have come to the place where my heart now longs for His presence, not His provision. Oh, I am not saying that I do not appreciate and enjoy all of His provisions in my life! Hardly! What I am saying is that I am finally in a place of rest in Him where I know that I know He is my provision. His provision for me is not something separate from His presence; it is in His presence that all my needs are met, satisfied, and made acceptable in His sight. I only long for Him. I long for Him to never leave me or forsake me. I long for Him to rest upon me, and cause me to lie down beside still waters and rest in Him.

So if He calls me to do something, then I will, for He will provide all that is needed to do so; but if He chooses to call our sons, or other sons or daughters to 'do something' then I rest in that also. It is truly not about me. It is about Him, His purpose, His will, His plan, and His rest. I will build Him a house of rest; yes, I will. That house is His house forever. That house is me, pure and simple. Me. Not a house built with hands, but an eternal house for Him to dwell within, and rest upon… that's me. I am His and He is mine. Will you declare this out of your own heart, too?

> *Make me Your house of rest,*
> *oh Lord.*

Ownership:

Lord, You know me. You know my heart. You know I, like David, had it in my heart to build many earthly things for You. I had it in my heart to build a house of rest for You and for the footstool of our God to be built by me also. I have spent my life making preparations to do those things that I thought would please You. But now I know that what pleases You is not necessarily what I do for You, but who I am for You. Lord, if You choose to use others to do those earthly things for You, Your earthly house, then I submit myself to You in every area. I rest in You and I long for You to rest in me. My heart's desire is to simply *be* with You; lead me beside the still waters, and cause me to lie down and rest with You. I am Your house, be in me, and I will be in You, in Jesus' name. Amen.

Action:

Lord, I ask You to know _____. Know _____'s heart. Lord, help _____ to learn how to be with You. Help (him/her) to know that it is in being in You, not doing for You, that (he/she) learns of You. I ask that You make _____ a place of rest for You. Be where _____ is. _____ longs to be at Your feet and for You to rest upon (him/her). I stand in the gap right now for _____ and I ask for You to move upon (his/her) heart to submit to Your perfect will for (his/her) life. Whether You ask (him/her) to build something here on this earth, or You ask (him/her) not to build something, may (he/she) be willing to obey You. Lead _____ beside the still waters and teach (him/her) how to rest in You, and for You to rest in (him/her). _____ will be Your house, be in _____, and (he/she) will be in You, in Jesus' name. Amen.

Be still ...

It is not what we do that matters to our God, but our obedience to His voice and plan that shows our heart towards Him. David wanted to do for the Lord. David was most probably a "type A/show me," type of guy. The Lord does not need our show. He just wants us. He wants me. He wants you. Are you willing to give yourself to Him? It is what He asks of you; it is what He requires of you. Be still and listen to His voice. Write down your deepest heart thoughts and desires.

_____

_____

_____

_____

_____

_____

_____

_____

_____

_____

_____

_____

_____

_____

_____

_____

_____

_____

_____

_____

_____

Day Thirty-Three

Luke 10:5-6
But whatever house you enter, first say, 'Peace to this house.'
"And if a son of peace is there, your peace will rest on it; if not, it will return to you.

Knowledge:

Have you ever gone over to someone's house and the moment you entered that home you were uncomfortable? Over the many years of traveling, I can tell you for sure, we have! I can tell you many things about the people who live in a house, just by the feeling in that house, the atmosphere and attitude of the house. Oh, don't get all up in arms about it! I am not talking spooky stuff here. I am talking practical observant things that anyone can utilize if you will look and listen.

Have you ever been invited to a home for dinner, and as you entered the home, there was so much commotion going on, so much noise, so much chaos that you wanted to turn around and run for the exit? Without even praying, it's not too hard to recognize the need for peace in that place! But notice the above scripture gives us a very clear clue as to why some homes are peaceful and others are not. If a son of peace is in the house, your peace will rest on it. In other words, if peace is not already residing in a place, the people who live there most probably will not accept the peace that resides in you. That does not mean that you lose your peace; you retain your peace as you leave the house, and your peace returns with you.

Many times we find ourselves in situations and circumstances where we do not have control over the 'feelings' or comfort of a place or position. It is not for us to be worried or fretful over this event. We are to walk in God's peace and allow His peace to rest upon us no matter what kind of situation we find ourselves in. I am a daughter of peace, and I have made it my goal in life to allow peace to rest upon, to make a tent upon my being.

I ask the Lord to cause peace to be within the walls of my house, and for rest to be the roof over me. *To rest upon me, means to tent upon, to cover, to reside on top of me!* Yes, rest covers me and peace surrounds me. There is nothing that comes or goes that has to affect me in a negative way, for God sets my perimeters!

Let's make a habit of not leaving our abode! Oh, I am not saying we are to 'hole up' in our houses. I am saying that wherever we go, whether near or far, to the corner for a gallon of milk, or across the country to visit family and friends, don't leave the house that the Lord has built! Don't stray from within your walls of peace and your roof of rest! Others have no right to change you, but you might be surprised how your presence could bring peace to their homes and lives.

So don't leave home without it... without what? Don't leave home without your spirit of peace, and your spirit of rest. Jesus is your foundation, peace fortifies your walls, and rest is your rooftop. You are covered!

Ownership:

Lord, I will go where You send me. My steps are ordered by Your Spirit. Wherever I go I will enter a house and say, *"Peace to this house."* If there is a person of peace living there, peace will then rest upon the house and those who reside in that house. If no one receives the peace and rest that I bring, then it will all return with me as I leave. I thank You, Father that You have given me Your Son, Jesus to be my foundation, peace to be the walls of my being, and for rest, Your rest to be the roof that covers my life daily, in Jesus' name. Amen.

Action:

Lord, I thank You that _____ will go where You send (him/her). _____'s steps are ordered by Your Spirit. Wherever _____ goes (he/she) will enter a house and say, *"Peace to this house."* If there is a person of peace living there, peace will then rest upon the house and those who reside in that house. If no one receives the peace and rest that _____ brings, then it will all return with (him/her) as (he/she) leaves. Thank You, Father that You have given _____ Your Son, Jesus, to be (his/her) foundation, peace to be the walls of (his/her) being, and for rest, Your rest to be the roof that covers _____'s life daily, in Jesus' name. Amen.

Be still ...

No matter where the day takes you, remember to stay in your house built by God, with Jesus as your foundation, peace as your walls, and rest as your rooftop. If He does not lead you there, then don't go. If He leads, enter with words of peace and expectancy. But no matter what happens, don't lose your own foundation, your walls, or the roof of your spiritual house. He loves you and longs for you to rest in Him.

When your house is built like this, you're covered!

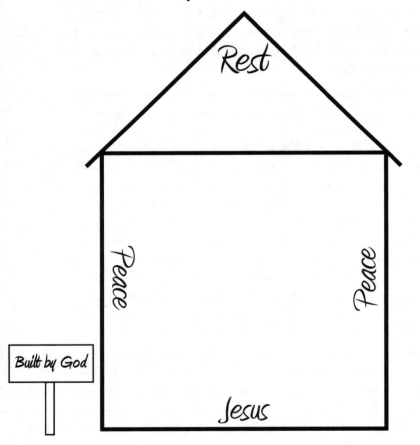

Rest

Peace

Peace

Built by God

Jesus

Entering Rest

Day Thirty-Four

Zechariah 1:10-11
And the man who stood among the myrtle trees answered and said, "These are the ones whom the Lord has sent to walk to and fro throughout the earth." So they answered the Angel of the Lord, who stood among the myrtle trees, and said, "We have walked to and fro throughout the earth, and behold, all the earth is resting quietly."

Knowledge:
When those whom the Lord has sent walk to and fro around you, your home, your daily life, and your being, what do they have to report back to the Lord? Have they seen all of your life and your being, resting quietly? Or is their report on you filled with the moments of doubt, fear, unbelief, despair, disappointment, discouragement, thoughts and even words of defeated attitudes and actions? It's not too late to change!

When our children were little, it seemed that keeping the house peaceful and at rest was quite a job, especially with personality plus children like we have! It's not that they were unruly; but they could be loud! I did not want to stifle their little personalities or energies but keeping the house and all of us in it, at rest and peace was very important to me. You can imagine, we played many versions of the Quiet Game! The children wanted to please me and when they would get a little rambunctious it would not be long until I heard, "Mama, I'm sorry," as they realized their voices and physical stunts had gone above the acceptable decibels for inside the house! Sometimes I would hear, "Mama, I'm sorry," almost in a sing-song throughout the day many times. I've mentioned this before, but it got to the point that I would answer back to the kids, "Don't be sorry, be different."

As I have gotten closer to the Lord over the years of serving and loving Him, I have found myself saying to Him, "Father, I'm sorry." He has never missed an opportunity to say back to my spirit, "Don't be sorry, be different." No matter what we have been doing, we don't have to be sorry, we can simply be different!

In Deuteronomy 12:9, the Bible states, *"...for as yet you have not come to the rest and the inheritance which the Lord your God is giving you."* We are on a journey to enter rest. It is a lifelong journey. Some days we are right on track; we are not distracted nor have we taken the wrong turn. Other days we seem to wander around, constantly saying how sorry we are for the choice we just made! Maybe we have not yet come to the rest, the full destination of rest that the Lord has for us, but we are entering this promised rest more every day. It is a wonderful promise from the Lord. It is an inheritance. Just think of that statement! One of the possessions we are to inherit is rest. The Bible is God's last will and testament. That's why we call it the Old and the New Testament. The Bible is God's will left here on the earth for those of us who are inheritors within the family! It is God's lasting will, never ending, never changing will! His will for me is to enter into rest and learn to live in rest, be in rest, stay in rest, and never leave it again. No matter what comes or goes in my life, rest is mine!

> *Thank You, Lord, for the blessings You have promised to me.*

To enter into God's kind of rest, and to learn to remain in this God ordained rest is to walk in the blessings of God Almighty! Read the Beatitudes, spoken by Jesus in Matthew 5:2-12, *Then He opened his mouth and taught them, saying:*

"Blessed are the poor in spirit, for theirs is the kingdom of heaven.

Blessed are those who mourn, for they shall be comforted.

Blessed are the meek, for they shall inherit the earth.

Blessed are those who hunger and thirst for righteousness, for they shall be filled.

Blessed are the merciful, for they shall obtain mercy.

Blessed are the pure in heart, for they shall see God.

Blessed are the peacemakers, for they shall be called sons of God.

Blessed are those who are persecuted for righteousness' sake, for theirs is the kingdom of heaven.

"Blessed are you when they revile and persecute you, and say all kinds of evil against you falsely for My sake.

"Rejoice and be exceedingly glad, for great is your reward in heaven, for so they persecuted the prophets who were before you.

As I read these wonderful, blessed promises, the Holy Spirit quickly pointed out to me that there is not one, "Blessed are the busy." Not one blessing for the busy! It's hard to believe that we can walk so closely to the Lord, and yet still be driven by the enemy of God to be so busy we don't have time to pray, or meditate, or even rest!! I can't imagine that I would ever wish this hectic lifestyle upon anyone, much less impose it upon myself!

Let's spend today meditating on the *rest* of God, not the list that we feel so compelled to keep crossing things off of in order to feel good about ourselves! Today, I meditate on resting in the Lord. Today, I trust Him only. I do not trust in myself, my own strength, riches, wealth, or anything else! I trust in the Lord with all my heart and I do not lean on my own understanding. I acknowledge Him, and Him only as the source of my strength and the source of my rest!

When the Lord's angels walk to and fro on the earth watching for those who are resting in Him, they will find me. Will they find you also? When they go to the throne of God to give an account of what we are doing for the kingdom, will they report that you are resting quietly in His presence and purpose for your life and future? Will they report that you have laid at His feet all futile exercises of self-imposed busy-ness that only produce works of the flesh? I pray the very report they give of you and me is one that when we stand before the Lord, He can say without hesitation, *"Well done, good and faithful servant; you have been faithful over a few things, I will make you ruler over many things. Enter into the joy of your lord."* (Matthew 25:23)

Ownership:

Lord, I pray for Your Spirit to teach me how to enter into Your rest. I long to hear You say to me, *"Well done, good and faithful servant; you have been faithful over a few things, I will make you ruler over many things. Enter into the joy of your lord."* I pray when the angel of the Lord gives an account of my daily life, he can say that I am resting quietly, at peace, and comfortable in my trust in You. I ask You Lord to teach me to walk as the blessed people in Your Word.

I am blessed when I am humble, for mine is the kingdom of heaven.

I am blessed when I mourn, for I shall be comforted.

I am blessed when I am meek, for I shall inherit the earth.

I am blessed when I hunger and thirst for righteousness, for I shall be filled.

I am blessed when I am merciful, for I shall obtain mercy.

I am blessed when my heart is pure, for I shall see God.

I am blessed when I am a peacemaker, for I shall be called the (son/daughter) of God.

I am blessed when I am persecuted for righteousness' sake, for the kingdom of heaven is mine.

I am blessed when others revile and persecute me, and say all kinds of evil against me falsely for Your sake, Lord.

I will rejoice and be exceedingly glad, for great is my reward in heaven, in Jesus' name. Amen.

Action:

Lord, I pray for Your Spirit to teach _____ how to enter into Your rest. May You say to _____, *"Well done, good and faithful servant.* _____ *has been faithful over a few things, I will make* _____ *ruler over many things.* _____ *will enter into the joy of the Lord."* I pray when the angel of the Lord gives an account of _____'s daily life he can say that _____ is resting quietly, at peace, and comfortable in (his/her) trust in You, Lord. I ask You, Lord, to teach _____ to walk as the blessed people in Your Word. I confess over _____ that _____ is blessed when (he/she) is humble, for (his/hers) is the kingdom of heaven.

_____ is blessed when (he/she) mourns, for (he/she) shall be comforted.

_____ is blessed when (he/she) is meek, for (he/she) shall inherit the earth.

_____ is blessed when (he/she) hungers and thirsts for righteousness, for (he/she) shall be filled.

_____ is blessed when(he/she) is merciful, for (he/she) shall obtain mercy.

_____ is blessed when (his/her) heart is pure, for (he/she) shall see God.

_____ is blessed when (he/she) is a peacemaker, for (he/she) shall be called the (son/daughter) of God.

_____ is blessed when (he/she) is persecuted for righteousness' sake, for the kingdom of heaven is (his/hers).

_____ is blessed when others revile and persecute (him/her), and say all kinds of evil against (him/her) falsely for Your sake, Lord.

_____ will rejoice and be exceedingly glad, for great is (his/her) reward in heaven, in Jesus' name. Amen.

Be still ...

Listen and obey. You belong to the kingdom of heaven; you are a part and portion of the kingdom of heaven. The kingdom of heaven is yours.

I pray that when the angel
of the Lord gives an account
of my daily life, he can say
that I am resting quietly,
at peace, and comfortable
in my trust in You,
my heavenly Father.

Day Thirty-Five

Proverbs 24:15-16
Do not lie in wait, O wicked man, against the dwelling of the righteous; Do not plunder his resting place; For a righteous man may fall seven times and rise again, but the wicked shall fall by calamity.

Job 24:22-23
But God draws the mighty away with His power; He rises up, but no man is sure of life. He gives them security, and they rely on it; Yet His eyes are on their ways.

I like the way it reads in the Amplified Bible.

Job 24:22-23
Yet [God] prolongs the life of the [wicked] mighty by His power; they rise up when they had despaired of life.
God gives them security, and they rest on it; and His eyes are upon their ways. (AMP)

Psalm 16:9
Therefore my heart is glad, and my glory rejoices; my flesh also will rest in hope.

Knowledge:
Over many years of learning how to rest in the Lord and stop the flesh toiling, striving, working that only produces flesh works... (sigh), I sadly realize that it has taken me too long to learn and too long to get to the place of entering God's rest. But I am learning now!

These years of studying and learning how to live out this

promise have caused me to notice the association of certain words. Here in three verses we can easily see the reference to the phrase, *"they rely on it,"* as the implication of the full statement and benefit of God's promise to mean that we can rest and rely on God to give us the security we need in Him. We can count on the fact that God is watching what we do because His eyes are on our ways, our daily going about with the regular walk of life.

We can thank God that the wicked man cannot come against our righteous dwelling and cannot plunder our resting place! What a wonderful promise from the Lord that even if I fall seven times as a righteous person of the Lord, I will rise again! It does not matter how many times I might be knocked down as long as the Lord is there, as He has promised to help me rise again! But the wicked will fall and stay down!

It would be so grand and even fun if the promise from the Lord was that we would never get knocked down in the first place, but that is not the promise. Most of our lives are a progressive journey of being knocked down, falling, and getting up. As I think about my life, and the many times I have fallen, spiritually, soulishly, and even physically, I cringe at the number of times! It is not a number I brag about, that's for sure!

I am thinking back to a season in my life when I was in college, and really felt the Lord leading me to be in pageants. Being a "type A/visionary," I assumed that when the Lord showed me that I was to be Miss America for His glory and His honor that I would win right away. I knew it had to be Him, and not me anyway, as there was nothing in my physical DNA that could cause me to be a pageant winner.

The first year I entered, I was a senior in high school, and since this was all God's idea, I assumed winning would be quick and easy. I was quickly "knocked down," as I lost the first year of entry into Miss Choctaw County. The following years were similar experiences of entering and losing. My freshman year at Mississippi State University, I entered the Miss MSU pageant and lost. My sophomore year, I entered the Miss MSU pageant and I lost. My junior year, I entered the Miss MSU pageant and I finally won a local pageant, only to proceed to the Miss Mississippi pageant that following summer and lose again! The more I entered and lost, the more I realized this pageant world quest was not about me at all.

It was not just that I was "knocked down" each year by losing the crowns, but I also had a literal knock down! I actually fell my junior year into the pavement, face first I might add, and scarred up my already scarred face, and broke off two of my front teeth, nearly at the root! Talk about falling down! All of these experiences did not teach me how to lose, nor did they teach me how to be knocked down. All these experiences taught me was how to get back up. Life is not about never having a problem, but when all the problems that can possibly come all seem to pile high and you can hardly find a place to catch your breath, that's when the winner inside of you, the God kind of winner that you were created to be, comes rising to the top! I learned more about winning from all those years of losing than I ever learned from finally 'winning the prize' and becoming Miss America, 1980! It is when we find ourselves in the dark, that the light can be clearly seen and followed.

> *When I get "knocked down" I will learn from it!*

I can truly say that my heart is glad and my glory rejoices for the more I know my victor, the sweeter the victory. I can rest in the future for I know that He only asks me to do what is impossible for me on my own. Then I can rest in Him, knowing that He must do the impossible while I simply rest in Him.

Ownership:

Lord, I thank You that the wicked man does not lie in wait against my righteous dwelling. The wicked will not plunder my resting place. I declare by Your Word that I am a righteous person and even when I fall over and over again, by Your strength I rise again. Lord, You give me security and rest as Your eyes are on my ways. Thank You, my Father, that I have a glad heart and a joyful countenance, and even my flesh will rest in Your hope, in Jesus' name. Amen.

Action:

Lord, I thank You that the wicked man does not lie in wait against _____ 's righteous dwelling. The wicked will not plunder _____ 's resting place. Thank You, Lord, that _____ is a righteous person and that Your Word says a righteous person may fall time and time again, but (he/she) will arise by Your strength. Lord, You give _____ security and rest as Your eyes are on (his/her) ways. Thank You, Father, that _____ has a glad heart and a joyful countenance, and even (his/her) flesh will rest in Your hope, in Jesus' name. Amen.

Be still ...

Smile to the Lord. Go on, no one is looking at you but Him. Can you have a joyful countenance because of His goodness? I believe you can! Spend a few quiet minutes with Him. He is the reason you can smile and be joyful, no matter what the circumstances or situation may be.

_____
_____
_____
_____
_____
_____
_____
_____
_____
_____
_____
_____
_____
_____
_____
_____
_____
_____
_____
_____
_____
_____
_____
_____
_____

Day Thirty-Six

Psalm 94:12-13
Blessed is the man whom You instruct, O Lord, and teach out of Your law, that You may give him rest from the days of adversity, until the pit is dug for the wicked.

Knowledge:

Each day as I write these words to you, my heart longs to be able to impart the power of Christ through these pages. Just the phrase, *"that You may give him rest from the days of adversity,"* causes my spirit to want to jump up and down in worship and praise! Don't we all long for the days when we have rest from adversity?

I remember a few summers ago, we had been through a surprising battle of the enemy through an unexpected surgery, recovery, a set back, and then recovery again. My thoughts go back even now to the big battle in my mind. The struggle each day was to overcome the nagging fear of 'waiting for the other shoe to drop.' Oh, you know what I mean, right? Harry and I had been plugging right along on our day in day out, week in week out, month in month out, routine of the decades of evangelism. We had become accustomed to our lives being paced by our preaching schedule.

As we would come home from a trip, the next few days were not spent resting and enjoying our family. Rather, these days were filled with the washing, repacking, working out the details and scheduling of the next trip, which was usually less than four days away with each return trip home. The worst part of it was, that way of living was the norm for us. It was all we knew. Our lives were marked by our traveling and preaching schedule. Many times in my prayer life I literally felt myself longing to plead with the Father to, "Stop the world; I want to get off!" But since this was the routine we were accustomed to, I didn't even know how to stop the cycle. Rest was not even in the thought life much less in the daily routine... or the weekly routine... or the monthly routine... or even the yearly routine!

It was a self-imposed lifestyle, with no one to blame but ourselves, me mostly, since I did most of the scheduling. I could never see the fault in it, until we had to stop. Without warning, a routine colonoscopy showed that I needed immediate surgery to have another section of my colon removed, all within a few days! Of course, I did not know how to stop, so we went right back on the road! Within two weeks of surgery, I was on the platform with my husband, preaching, teaching, singing and worshiping the Lord.

A few short weeks later, I was literally carried by our two sons into the emergency room in the middle of the night with a twisted colon, which proved to be one of the most painful experiences of my entire life! And yes, it was during this season that I began hearing the Lord say, "Be still. Be still. Be still." I wanted to listen and obey. I wanted to stop the world and get off, but I truly did not know how. We pushed through a few more months, with the Lord ever gently urging me to a place of stillness and rest. A continual, "Be still," were the words from my Father's lips to my stubborn ears.

After a few months of trying to continue on, there was such an onslaught of the adversary's attacks, from Harry's mom having a stroke, to my step-dad suddenly dying of a heart attack, to illness attacking our sons and us almost continually. Finally, Harry said to me while we were preaching in the Midwest, "When we get home you are cancelling the calendar until further notice." I was stunned in my natural mind and more than a little disturbed and yet I knew Harry had heard the Lord and was obeying His voice.

I agreed to call all our dates for the following three months, and 'postpone' them until a later time, as the word 'cancel' just would not come out of my mouth! I re-arranged the schedule and the most amazing part was it was so easy. The Lord directed our steps, and each call I made was with ease and received with grace and mercy, love and appreciation for our obedience. Even so, I could not help but feel as though I was still, 'waiting for the other shoe to drop.'

As we approached the throne of God in prayer for literally hours a day, I had the most heavy 'thing' hanging on me, trying to convince me in my mind that this was not over, that we had only begun to have problems, that we had not seen anything yet, etc. Finally, one day in prayer, I verbalized to the Lord this foreboding and hovering spirit of dread that was trying to hold my mind captive. I came right out with it and I said, "In the name of Jesus, you spirit of 'waiting for the other shoe to drop,' you must go, in Jesus' name!"

Well, there it was, out in the open. No hovering around in the darkness trying to force thoughts in to keep me in torment! There it was all out there for everybody to see. God and everybody! Once the words were spoken in the name of Jesus and the authority had been taken in His name, the 'thing' lost its power. Oh, it continued to try to hold its position for several more days but it had lost its power in the light of the glory of God.

So if any kind of tormenting adversary has been hanging out around your thinking, you can do just like I did. In the name of Almighty Jesus Christ, tell it to go, and don't come back! There were no more 'shoes to drop' as we entered into the 'be still and know that He is God' mode and we refused to come out!

> *Resting in You is vital to my life.*
> *I will stubbornly guard our time*
> *together, Jesus.*

Ownership:

Lord, I thank You for the authority and power You have given me through the name of my Savior and Lord, Jesus the Christ! I thank You that I am blessed because I receive my instruction from You, Lord. You teach me out of Your law that You may give me rest from the days of adversity. Thank You, my Father, that I have rest from the adversary and I will not sit around with the dread of waiting for the 'other shoe to drop.' The only thing I am waiting for, Lord, is for the pit to be dug for the wicked. Until then, I rest in You, I adore You, and I love You more each day, in Jesus' name. Amen.

Action:

Lord, I thank You for _____ to take the authority and power given to (him/her) by You through the name of Jesus the Christ! I thank You that _____ is blessed because (he/she) receives instruction from You, Lord. You teach _____ out of Your law that You, Lord, may give _____ rest from the days of adversity. Thank You, Father, that _____ has rest from the adversary and _____ will not sit around with the dread of waiting for the 'other shoe to drop' syndrome. The only thing that _____ waits for is for the pit to be dug for the wicked. _____ rests in You, in the name of Jesus. Amen.

Be still ...

Take every thought captive and command the adversary to leave you. The enemy and adversary cannot stay in the presence of Almighty God and He is here with you. Be still and listen.

_____

_____

_____

_____

_____

_____

_____

_____

_____

_____

_____

_____

_____

_____

_____

_____

_____

_____

_____

_____

_____

_____

_____

_____

_____

_____

_____

Spirit of the Lord,
come upon me
and make me
a different
person!

Day Thirty-Seven

Numbers 11:25-26
Then the Lord came down in the cloud, and spoke to him, and took of the Spirit that was upon him, and placed the same upon the seventy elders; and it happened, when the Spirit rested upon them, that they prophesied, although they never did so again. But two men had remained in the camp; the name of one was Eldad, and the name of the other Medad. And the Spirit rested upon them. Now they were among those listed, but who had not gone out to the tabernacle; yet they prophesied in the camp.

Knowledge:

It can be amazing when the Spirit of the Lord decides to rest upon any of us! It can cause quite a stir! Oh, how I long for the Spirit of the Lord to rest upon me, to take up residence, 'tenting' upon me! I long to go about my daily business and cause the kind of stir that Eldad and Medad caused on that day.

When I found this scripture about the Spirit of the Lord actually resting upon human flesh, I got so excited, for isn't this what we all want in our lives, and on our lives? As I read the entire chapter, the story reminded me that many times the change that occurs and the passion and zeal that comes upon us by the Spirit of God resting on us, can cause those around us to be uncomfortable! It was no different for Eldad and Medad. When the Spirit of the Lord rested upon them, they began to prophesy and had no problem doing so throughout the camp! These two men were elders but were not present in the tabernacle when the Spirit of the Lord had rested upon the other elders.

Those elders who were present in the tabernacle during that impartation of the Spirit of God had prophesied only that one time.

But Eldad and Medad were not even present in the tabernacle and yet the Spirit of the Lord rested upon them also! The Spirit of the Lord can find you wherever you are, and rest upon you, and cause you to be different! We can't control the place of the Holy Spirit's resting! Many times the Spirit of God chooses the most unlikely of candidates on which to rest! I am definitely one of those unlikely candidates, from a poor, farming background in Choctaw County, Mississippi, and yet the Spirit of the Lord rested upon me, and still does.

Holy Spirit,
rest upon me...
You are welcome
in my life.

If you read the entire 11th chapter in the book of Numbers, you will find that in the following verses, Joshua was not happy about these two men going around the camp prophesying and he ran to Moses and asked him to make them stop! But Moses, longing for more of God at all times, said in verse 29, *"...Are you zealous for my sake? Oh, that all the Lord's people were prophets and that the Lord would put His Spirit upon them!"*

My heart wants to cry out like Moses did, with passion and zeal for more outpouring of God's Spirit upon all flesh. I want to cry out right now to the Lord, "Oh, that all the Lord's people were prophets and that the Lord would put His Spirit upon them! Lord, pour out Your Spirit upon all flesh; cause us to prophesy from Your mouth to the ears of Your people. Let us not be so concerned about what other people would think of us, but only be concerned with obeying You, being filled with Your presence to the point of perpetual prophecy pouring forth from our lips to the ears of those who need to desperately hear a word from You, Lord!"

In I Samuel 16:23, *"And so it was, whenever the spirit from God was upon Saul, that David would take a harp and play it with his hand. Then Saul would become refreshed and well, and the distressing spirit would depart from him."* Before this instance in Saul and David's lives, in I Samuel 10:6, the Lord used His Spirit to change Saul. The verse reads this way, *"Then the Spirit of the Lord will come upon you, and you will prophesy with them and be turned into another man."* Oh, that the Spirit of the Lord would come upon us all and turn us into different people! Lord, let this be so for all of us to be more like You, and less like ourselves. This is the power of the Spirit of the Lord! It can cause us to become different people!

Ownership:

Lord, I ask You to allow Your Spirit to come upon me, change me, and transform me. Cause me to become a different person than my old self. Thank You, that when I received Jesus Christ as my Lord and Savior that my old man died, and I took on a new image, for eternity, the very image and likeness of Jesus Christ, my Lord. Lord, I ask for the Holy Spirit to come down upon me and rest upon me. Tent over me, Spirit of God, make me Your resting place. I will dwell with Your Spirit from this day forth. May Your Holy Spirit dwell with me, and on me today and always. Use me, Lord, to prophesy, to speak forth Your words to all those lives around me each and every day. Teach me how to speak Your words with love, compassion, and mercy, just as Jesus did while He was on the earth. Teach me to be an extension of Jesus through Your Spirit resting upon me. I yield my life, my steps, my thoughts and my words to You, in Jesus' name. Amen.

Action:

Lord, I ask You to allow Your Spirit to come upon _____, change _____, and transform _____. Cause _____ to become a different person than (his/her) old self. Thank You, that when _____ (receives/received) Jesus Christ as (his/her) Lord and Savior that (his/her) old person died, and _____ took on a new image, for eternity, the very image and likeness of Jesus Christ, (his/her) Lord. Lord, I ask for the Holy Spirit to come down upon _____ and rest upon (him/her). Tent over _____, Spirit of God, and make (him/her) Your resting place. _____ will dwell with Your Spirit from this day forth. May Your Holy Spirit dwell with _____, and on _____ today and always. Use _____, Lord, to prophesy, to speak forth Your words to all those lives around (him/her) each and every day. Teach _____ how to speak Your words with love, compassion, and mercy, just as Jesus did while He was on the earth. Teach _____ to be an extension of Jesus through Your Spirit resting upon _____. Lord, move upon _____ even now to yield (his/her) life, steps, thoughts and words to You, in Jesus' name. Amen.

Be still ...

Just sit and listen. Learn from your Father God, through the Holy Spirit resting upon your very being.

_____

_____

_____

_____

_____

_____

_____

_____

_____

_____

_____

_____

_____

_____

_____

_____

_____

_____

_____

_____

_____

_____

_____

_____

_____

_____

_____

_____

_____

Day Thirty-Eight

Exodus 24:16-17
Now the glory of the Lord rested on Mount Sinai, and the cloud covered it six days. And on the seventh day he called to Moses out of the midst of the cloud. The sight of the glory of the Lord was like a consuming fire on the top of the mountain in the eyes of the children of Israel.

Knowledge:

I long for the glory of the Lord to rest upon me as it rested on Mount Sinai. I look for the cloud to cover me for my entire life, not just six days. But these numbers are very important to fully understand this passage of scripture. *Six* is a very important number for mankind. It is the day of the week that mankind was created in the beginning. It is the *waw* in the Hebrew numerical/alphabet system which has the meaning *hook*. The number *six* stands for *the weakness of man, the evils of Satan, and the manifestation of sin* according to Dr. Ed Vallowe in the book, *Biblical Mathematics, Keys to Scripture Numerics.*[2] Dr. Vallowe states that as the number seven was the sacred number to the Jews, the number six fell short of it and failed, thus standing for the full measure of manifested sin for mankind.

Man was created on the sixth day. Once mankind fell to the power of sin, it was appointed to man to labor for six days each week. The Hebrew slave was to serve for six years. The land was to be sown for six years and then to rest the seventh year. The kingdoms of this world are to last for six thousand years. In the above scripture we can see where Moses was compelled to wait six days before

God called to him. But on the seventh day, Moses heard the voice of the Lord and he saw the sight of the glory of the Lord, like a consuming fire on the top of the mountain! And he was not the only one who saw this all-consuming fire; it was seen in the eyes of the children of Israel. An entire nation of people saw the glory of the Lord as an all-consuming fire! Oh, how I wish I could have seen that! But I will see it someday, and I pray it is very soon! In the meantime, I welcome the all-consuming fire of the Lord to rest upon me! Lord, sit upon me with Your purifying and all-consuming fire!

As negative in connotation as the number six is, the number *seven* is just that positive. In the Hebrew alphabet the seventh letter/number is *zayin* which means *weapon.* In Dr. Vallowe's numbers book[2], he describes *seven* as *the number for completeness, spiritual, and perfection.* The last three written, recorded words that we have of the Father God speaking is in Genesis 2, when God the Father said, *"It is finished."* Those same three words were the last said by the Son, Jesus Christ on the cross, *"It is finished." It means it is done, completed, finished, perfected, all things spiritual are!* Are what? All things spiritual are done, completed, finished, perfected. I Am, that I Am has finished what He started!

Just as Satan has tried to use the number *six* as a hook in mankind's mouth, leading humanity away from the throne of God, God uses the number *seven* as a weapon against Satan and all his fallen cohorts. When God said through His mouth, His Word, His Son, and now His bride, *"It is finished."* He meant it! It is finished.

The consuming fire in the above verse represents the purging power of God's glorious presence on humanity. When

> *Purge me,*
> *Purify me,*
> *Complete me,*
> *oh Lord!*

we allow the Lord to purge us with His fire, and consume everything within us that is not like Him, we are learning to rest in Him, trusting Him to complete and perfect what He has started in us. Philippians 1:6 states that, *"...He who has begun a good work in you will complete it until the day of Jesus Christ."*

God the Father has begun a good work in you, and He is faithful to complete what He has started. In fact, in the realm of the spiritual, the supernatural, the realm of true reality, not this world which the Bible calls a vapor... in the realm and timetable that counts, God's realm - this is what He says about you. He has already finished what He has started in you. So you don't stop, you don't quit. You are not having to 'do' anything. Jesus already did it, God, the Father, already finished it. Your job is to rest in it, seeing His glory come down upon you forever!

Ownership:

Lord, I thank You that it is Your glory I long for, not my own. I ask that Your glory rest upon me, and that Your rest cover me all my days upon this earth. I thank You, Father, that by Your Word, You have finished in me and for me the completed image of who You are. I thank You, Lord, that I have eyes to see in the realm of the spirit and I see Your glory like a consuming fire upon my life. Purify me, Lord, and create within me a pure heart to serve and love You, in Jesus' name. Amen.

Action:

Lord, I thank You that it is Your glory that _____ longs for, and not (his/her) own. I ask that Your glory rest upon _____, and that Your rest covers _____ all the days of (his/her) life. Thank You, Father, that by Your Word, You have finished in _____ and for (him/her) the completed and perfected image of who You are.   Thank You, Lord, that _____ has eyes to see in the spirit realm and that (he/she) sees Your glory like a consuming fire upon (his/her) life. Purify _____, Lord, and create within (him/her) a pure heart to serve and love You, in Jesus' name. Amen.

Philippians 1:6

"... He who has begun a good work in you shall complete it until the day of Jesus Christ;"

Be still ...

Ask the Lord to send forth His purifying and cleansing presence as you pray and seek His face.

_____

_____

_____

_____

_____

_____

_____

_____

_____

_____

_____

_____

_____

_____

_____

_____

_____

_____

_____

_____

_____

_____

_____

_____

_____

_____

_____

_____

_____

_____

_____

_____

_____

_____

Day Thirty-Nine

Genesis 2:1-2
Thus the heavens and the earth, and all the host of them, were finished. And on the seventh day God ended His work which He had done, and He rested on the seventh day from all His work which He had done.

Knowledge:

It is finished… well, not quite. We have two more days to go before we can honestly say we have finished learning to enter into God's kind of rest. Are you almost there? Do you feel like you are actually reaching the destination of rest? You should be feeling this way, and thinking this way for as a person thinks in his or her heart so is he or she. (Proverbs 23:7) Hopefully, by now your thinking has begun to shift more in line with who you are, not what you do. For instance, let's say you meet someone new, introductions are made, and you say, "Tell me about yourself," instead of, "What do you do?" Hopefully, we have taken a giant step forward to look for more in people than what they do, but to try to discover who they really are. And with this great paradigm shift in our thinking, we should also be able to display to those we meet, and to those with whom we are in contact each day, not just what we do, but who we really are.

Our focus should be more along the lines of our 'being' rather than on our 'doing.' With those kinds of radical adjustments in our thought patterns and conversations, we should be realizing that our earth walk is much more than what we do. Our earth's existence should be based upon who we are, from the inside out. One morning while Harry and I were in prayer, during one of those contemplative discussions, I said to Harry, "The only thing I want written on the headstone of my grave is, 'She prayed.'"

He looked at me with that, "You're way out there on that limb again this morning," kind of look that I must admit I see quite often. But I went on to explain that as we had written this book together and spent so much time studying and praying over the past 22 months on this subject of rest, I realized the only important thing that I have learned to do that has any real and lasting effect for generations to come is that I have learned to pray. Please notice that I did not use the wording, "how to pray," for prayer is not a how-to, which would indicate prayer being more of a ritual, a religious act or practice. Prayer is not about the how-to's, which come and go with each new idea and thought of another type A personality author. Prayer is intimacy in its truest form. Prayer is a way of life, a deep and personal relationship between a *human being* and the ultimate one and only true *Almighty God being ... I AM.* So when my life is over and all is said and done, please make sure if anyone speaks of me, they remember one thing, "She prayed."

> *I want to know God's thoughts;*

> *all else are details.*
> *- Einstein*

Albert Einstein once said, "I want to know God's thoughts; all else are details."

Oh how true this is. What possibly could we think we could know apart from God's thoughts? When I learn to enter His rest, then I can rest in Him. All else are details.

God seems to do everything in groups of three. The Father God's last words were, *"It is finished."* Jesus Christ, the Son of God's last words were, *"It is finished."* So who is the third? The Holy Spirit must finish the circle of three, but He can only speak through the voice of humanity. Revelation 22:17 gives us the words to say that agree with the Father and the Son, *"And the Spirit and the bride say, 'Come!'"* With this invitation to the bridegroom to come and receive His bride, the bride then finds her voice to finish for all mankind the circle of the, "It is finished," statements. We say it loud and clear when we say, "Come!" It is finished.

Ownership:

Lord, I ask You to help me change the way I think. I have been programmed by the world around me to think like the world, but I ask You to teach me to think like You so that I can be like You. Your Word tells me that how I think affects who I am; so Lord, help me to know Your thoughts. I want to know Your thoughts. Teach me to get over myself and to put my focus on the finish line of this earth race. I long to enter Your kind of kingdom living while I am here on this earth. Lord, I long to declare that I am at the end of myself, and it is finished. Help me to do this by Your Word and in Your will, in Jesus' name. Amen.

Action:

Lord, I ask You to help _____ change the way (he/she) thinks. _____ has been programmed by the world around (him/her) to think like the world, but I ask You to teach _____ to think like You, so (he/she) can be like You. Your Word tells us that how _____ thinks affects who _____ is; so Lord, help _____ to know Your thoughts, which in turn, will help (him/her) to know You more. _____ wants to know Your thoughts. Teach (him/her) to get over (himself/herself) and to put (his/her) focus on the finish line of this earth race. Help _____ to long to enter Your kind of kingdom living while here on this earth. Lord, help _____ to declare that (he/she) is at the end of (himself/herself), and it is finished. Help _____ to do this by Your Word and in Your will, in Jesus' name. Amen.

Revelation 22:13
Jesus said,
"I am the
Alpha and the Omega,
the Beginning and the End,
the First and the Last."

Be still ...

You are nearing the end of this forty-day journey and one thing is becoming clear. To move into the rest that the Lord has ordained for you, you must learn how to leave your 'self' behind, and push toward the finish line of His way of thinking and being. It truly is all about Him... to have His rest, means we must have Him. To have all of Him, means we must be empty of ourselves. Are there a few more things you need to pour out of your 'self' to make more room for Him and His presence?

_____

_____

_____

_____

_____

_____

_____

_____

_____

_____

_____

_____

_____

_____

_____

_____

_____

_____

_____

_____

_____

Day Forty

Genesis 2:3-4
Then God blessed the seventh day and sanctified it, because in it He rested from all His work which God had created and made. This is the history of the heavens and the earth when they were created, in the day that the Lord God made the earth and the heavens...

Knowledge:

Entering God's rest is such a simple act of following Him. God blessed the seventh day and set it apart, sanctified it, because in the seventh day God rested from all His work which He had created and made. What's my part in all of this? I am to follow the Lord into His rest. Mankind was made on the last day, at the end of the day. So when God blessed the seventh day, He blessed our rest day; He blessed our rest.

> REST is ordained by God. He planned it and promised it!

I find it quite interesting that Genesis 2:4 begins with *"This is the history of the heavens and the earth..."*. When is history recorded? At the beginning? Of course not! If it is history then it has already happened, and it is finished! So the Bible then is the history of the heavens and the earth. The Bible is history! It is finished! God is not writing this as He goes along! He's not writing the chapters of your life as you live a little at a time! Before the earth began, God knew you. You were already finished, and even your history had already been written!

Psalm 22:31 states, *"They will come and declare His righteousness to a people who will be born, that He has done this."* Okay, this sentence is a verb disagreement from beginning to end! In one sentence we have future, *"they will come,"* present tense, *"and declare,"* future again, *"to a people who will be born,"* and ultimately past tense, *"that He has done this."* How is this even possible? Because inside of God there is no such thing as past, present, and future. In God, He is. He told Moses to tell the people, "I AM." Inside of the very essence and presence of Almighty God, we are finished, even before we have begun this earth's existence!

So what does this all have to do with entering rest? It has everything to do with it! When we finally relax and enjoy the ride of life, the journey with the Lord, the intimate and deep pleasure of His presence and purpose that He has already finished, we can turn loose of the "death grip" we have on our day in and day out lives. We can never enter God's kind of rest until we ultimately give up having to be in control. Our destiny is already set inside of God, therefore, we can give it up and enjoy His presence!

If I could open up your head and pour into you the impartation of entering this God-given position of rest I would! I did not find this easily but I could have, if I would have only stopped long enough to listen and obey. It has taken me too long to get here, but praise God, I am here now. I am entering rest, God's rest. I recognize this is His promise to all, but only a few will enter in. I will enter His rest. I will to do so. I commit to do so. I will not get on the hamster wheel in the little cage of life any more! I not only thank God for knocking me off the wheel, I ask Him to keep me knocked off the wheel! No longer do I start my prayer with, "Lord, stop the world; I want to get off!"

He has called me, and I obey. So can you, but you must choose to do so. No one can make you, but the benefits are more than you can ever imagine! In the early 1990's, I was preaching a message on rest, and I told a story about a little girl. This little girl was learning to ride a bicycle and her father was teaching her. She finally got the balancing part, and the pedaling, and the steering figured out. She recognized that at first she could only do it when her father steadied her, and pushed her along; but little by little she began to put all the components together of the intricacies of riding her bike. She really had it down. She did great in the front yard, and even better going down the driveway. But the real test was in the back yard, as there was a very long, tall hill.

The little girl and her father maneuvered the bicycle up the hill, and as he steadied her atop the bike, her father reminded her of the lessons she had learned. He went over in detail all the tips and pointers he had taught her throughout the day. He finished his last lesson to her with a reminder to remember the most important lesson of all. She looked up into his eyes and with the most assurance any little girl can give her father, she smiled and said she remembered it all.

The father made his way to position himself about halfway down the hill. He let his daughter know that He was in position and that she could push off and come down the hill. There she came, picking up speed as she quickly approached her father. Her eyes widened as she got closer and closer and quickly passed him by. He could see the terror in her eyes and see the tenseness in her body. He instinctively knew that she had forgotten the greatest lesson of all. As she approached the bottom of the hill now with uncontrollable speed that was so far out of her expertise in bicycle riding, her father heard her scream, "Daddy, Daddy, help me! I forgot how to stop!" Of course, we all know what happened, and why do we know so well? Because we have all been just like this little girl in life. We learned all the lessons of how to *go* but we forgot to listen when the lesson of how to *stop* was being taught.

God's seventh day, set apart to rest, was mankind's first full day on earth. God ordained and created us to rest and be with Him. He made us, but not because He needed us to do anything. He created us because He wanted to be with us. Have we gotten so busy in our doing, even those of us who do for the kingdom, that we have forgotten why we were created? He wants you; He wants me; He wants us.

Exodus 33:14 states that the Lord said, *"My Presence will go with you, and I will give you rest."* It is in being with Him that we find what we long for, and what we need. We need His presence and we need His rest.

Are you like the little girl? Are you uncontrollably careening downhill, so fast that a crash is inevitable? Your Father God has positioned Himself on the hill! He is waiting to catch you and hold you. Simply call out to Him now. Tell Him you forgot the most important lesson of all. You forgot how to stop. He is waiting ... shhh, be still.

Ownership:

Lord, I acknowledge my failure of entering Your promise of rest. Your Word said that only a few would enter in. Lord, even if I am the only one, I want to obey You. I trust You to accomplish more through my obedience of entering rest, than in my own pursuits of trying to do things on my own. Lord, forgive me for all the flesh works that I have done in my lifetime. Teach me how to not run ahead of You, but to stay right with You. When You move, Lord, then I will move. When You stop, Lord, then I will stop. As Ruth said to Naomi, *"Wherever you go, I will go."* (Ruth 1:16). Lord, I do not want to be far from You anymore. I have spent a lifetime learning how to make lists, write goals, and live by rules and laws. Lord, I'm done. It is finished. I am Your bride and I say, *"Come!"* in Jesus' name. Amen.

Action:

Lord, for my precious one whom You love so much, for _____ I stand in the gap right now. By Your Spirit, speak to _____ and show (him/her) the need to slow down and listen to You. Teach _____ to trust You to accomplish more through obedience of entering rest, than in (his/her) pursuits of trying to do things on (his/her) own. Lord, forgive _____ for all the flesh works that (he/she) has done in (his/her) lifetime. Teach _____ how to not run ahead of You, but to stay right with You. When You move, Lord, then _____ will move. When You stop, Lord, then _____ will stop. As Ruth said to Naomi, *"Wherever you go, I will go."* (Ruth 1:16). Lord, keep _____ close to You, and don't let (him/her) get too far away. _____ has spent a lifetime learning how to make lists, write goals, and live by rules and laws. Lord, _____ is done. By faith, I call this so. It is finished. _____ is Your bride and _____ says, *"Come!"* in Jesus' name. Amen.

Be still ...

Here is your opportunity to never leave this place again. Enter rest; it's your promise. God promised you this place of rest, so don't take it for granted... go on in, He is waiting.

_____

_____

_____

_____

_____

_____

_____

_____

_____

_____

_____

_____

_____

_____

_____

_____

_____

_____

_____

_____

_____

_____

_____

_____

_____

_____

_____

_____

_____

_____

You have completed this forty-day commitment to reading, studying, praying and journaling, but please don't think your journey ends here! There is so much more to this amazing expedition - this incredible, life-changing discovery of rest!

He is readily available to you and to me - and He makes sure that we find Him when we seek Him. But we do have to seek Him!

Proverbs 8:17
I love those who love me, And those who seek me diligently will find me.

I believe that you will experience an overwhelmingly rich and rewarding "love-awakening" as you pursue your Creator with all your might! It was worth it to Him to undergo torment and death on the cross - for you. Make it worth your time and effort to pursue HIM and see where He takes you as you journey toward . . .

Entering Rest.

If you feel the Holy Spirit prompting you, give this book to the one you dedicated it to in the beginning. You have journeyed with them in your prayers for forty days; now give them the gift of this discovery journey.

If this book has been your own private diary between you and your heavenly Father, then read it again, and often! It will bless you through the years, to meditate on the intimate times of honesty and reflection that He led you to, and also on the victories...
that He led you through!

Prayer of Salvation

If you have never made Jesus the Lord of your life, or if you would like to re-dedicate your life to Him, please pray this prayer of salvation.

Heavenly Father, I come to You admitting that I am a sinner. Right now, I choose to turn away from sin and I ask You to cleanse me of all unrighteousness. I believe that Your Son, Jesus, died on the cross to take away my sins. I also believe that He rose again from the dead so that I can be forgiven of my sins and be made righteous though faith in Him. I call upon the name of Jesus Christ to be the Lord and Savior of my life. Jesus, I choose to follow You and I ask that You fill me with the power of the Holy Spirit. I declare right now that I am a child of God! I am free from sin and full of the righteousness of God. I am saved, in Jesus' name. Amen.

Please contact us to let us know you prayed this prayer!

Salem Family Ministries
PO Box 701287
Tulsa, Oklahoma 74170
www.salemfamilyministries.org

Please include your prayer requests
and comments when you write.

About the Authors

Harry and Cheryl Salem travel the world ministering the gospel, telling people that Jesus loves them and that He is returning soon! Their lives revolve around seeking the Lord and where He would have them go. Two by two they travel, loving God's people, living and moving in His anointing.

In 1999, Harry and Cheryl endured the loss of their 6 year old daughter, Gabrielle. As they boldly took steps of faith to overcome the agonizing pain of Gabrielle's death, they asked God to restore them and for souls to come into His kingdom. God has restored the Salem family and because of His mighty anointing, the altars have been full! Harry and Cheryl are committed to leading godly lives as an example to others. Their two sons, Harry III and Roman, are continuing their education in addition to participating in the family ministry.

Together, Harry and Cheryl have written books and produced numerous music and ministry CDs to help enable believers, to not only overcome but to excel in their Christian lives.

They love people and they love pouring themselves out because God's immense mercy, grace and love keeps them filled up in return. They are blessed and privileged to go out, two by two, reaching families one by one. (Luke 10:1-2)

Harry & Cheryl Salem

For more information, visit
www.salemfamilyministries.org

Other Available Books

Rebuilding the Ruins of Worship
We Who Worship
The Rise of an Orphan Generation: Longing for a Father
The Presence of Angels in Your Life
Don't Kill Each Other! Let God Do It!
Obtaining Peace - A 40-Day Prayer Journal
2 Becoming 1
The Choice is Yours
Overcoming Fear - A 40-Day Prayer Journal
Every Body Needs Balance
From Grief to Glory
From Mourning to Morning
Distractions from Destiny
Speak the Word Over Your Family for Finances
Speak the Word Over Your Family for Healing
Speak the Word Over Your Family for Salvation
*Covenant Conquerors**
Warriors of the Word
*Fight in the Heavenlies**
*It's Too Soon to Give Up**
Being #1 at Being #2
For Men Only
*An Angel's Touch**
A Royal Child
The Mommy Book
*How to Get a Balanced Body**
*Simple Facts; Salvation, Healing & the Holy Ghost**
*Health & Beauty Secrets**
*Choose to be Happy**
Abuse ... Bruised but not Broken
You Are Somebody
A Bright Shining Place - The Story of a Miracle

*Call for availability

References

[1]Strong, James. *Abingdon's Strong's Exhaustive Concordance of the Bible* (Nashville: Abingdon, 1980).

[2]Vallowe, Ed. *Biblical Mathematics - Keys to Scripture Numerics* (The Olive Press, 20th Printing, © 1998).

Please note:
To those of you who read this book or any of our books, the views and opinions expressed are based on our personal lives and our interpretation of the Bible.